# The Big Wheel

*Bruce Thomas*

Faber and Faber
BOSTON LONDON

**Library of Congress Cataloging-in-Publication Data**

Thomas, Bruce.
    The big wheel / Bruce Thomas.
        p.      cm.
    "First published in the United Kingdom in 1990 by Viking, the Penguin Group"—T.p. verso.
    ISBN 0-571-12944-7 (pbk.) : $10.95
    1. Thomas, Bruce. 2. Rock musicians—Biography. I. Title.
ML419.T45A3      1991
782.42166'092'2—dc20                                             91-22329
[B]                                                                   CIP


For permission to reproduce copyright material, the author and publisher gratefully acknowledge Peer-Southern Music for lyric from "Long Tall Sally" by Blackwell, Penniman and Johnson.


Cover design by Mary Maurer
Cover photograph by Steven Nilsson

Printed in the United States of America

*For Suzanne*

Dear Miss Manners,
What do you consider a good conversation opener?

Gentle Reader,
Almost anything except: 'I've been on a wonderful journey of self-discovery lately, and I'd like to share it with you.'

From *Miss Manners' Guide to Excruciatingly Good Behaviour*

# Foreword

It would be the perfect place to go mad. Anywhere this bare does not feel secure or predictable: you can only watch the road for so long before you're absorbed. You go for mile after mile that you know you will never remember – sitting blind, sitting dumb and knowing nothing – neither asleep nor awake, neither there nor here. Then suddenly you reappear, forced to pay attention, because in all the unseen vastness you are the only life that can prove its own existence and because the only real movement and change is that which is going on in your own little world. At last, just when you begin to think that the road can go no further, it goes further – mile after mile, on and on, straight and ahead. No longer running out of the past and into the future, the road is always here: always present. Clock time doesn't pass here any more. Now we are passing through time . . .

The mile markers went on and on as the road became flatter and ever more featureless. The grey blanket that was overhead an hour ago had been drawn back to reveal a dark-steel sheet of sky washed and wiped clean of anything. The sky had darkened so much that the big semis coming the other way had their lights on full and even their bright chromework looked dull. This was one of the most desolate strips of road in America, and there was plenty of competition. The rain had made it a ribbon of grey shades that held all the reflections so that even the light appeared to be made out of concrete.

This was dead, level country that you could do nothing but drive through. It unfolded into a slowly changing continuum of dull impressions that brought half-hearted responses. It stretched out so that nothing, apart from a few missile silos, could be hidden away. If ever those missiles were launched the whole world would end up looking like this. The accidental geometry of huge rock formations against the sky exposed, rather than relieved, the incredible emptiness. The shapes, in silhouette, were almost abstract. They changed according to the speed we travelled, but always too slowly. The big, dramatic vista continually promised, or threatened, something momentous that never happened.

I sat there, determined that the ride – the story of the journey – should have some structure, anything other than a random and pointless series of memories, comments and hopes that might begin to play on the nerves. Meanwhile, interest continued under its own momentum to fix on anything it found remotely interesting: an abandoned car, beer cans, a billboard, a piece of trash, a dead animal.

Other than the road itself and the single strand of telephone wire, there were no signs of man. This place belonged to something else. The mood of bleakness that was descending on me was in response to my feeling completely at the mercy of the surroundings, the shapes and blobs and strips of dull colour, that wormed their way into my psyche so that the difference between the inner landscape and the outer world gradually was becoming more and more blurred. Slowly I was being unhinged by the excess of nothing: with no way of putting things into scale, the mind fumbled to grasp what it saw.

It was a landscape that some kind of movement of the mind alone could interrupt. Slowly it revealed in me what normally lay covered up, in all the usual noisy and busy places. Having no sense of place was beginning to unravel just a little sense of self. The road keeps driving you back into this enforced meditation and, like an ascetic in the desert, all you find is your own imagination. Sometimes you follow it and sometimes you get lost in it. Your eyelids begin to droop. Where have you been? Asleep? Or dead? You may as well have been. And then you pick up the thread of remembering, the silver strand, the single telephone wire running along beside.

Another two hundred uninterrupted miles threw up more images from sci-fi movies, or brought memories of ancient ruins: moonscapes and bombsites, fiction and fact, real and imaginary. Past events, the dull sensation of the present and imagination were all hopelessly mixed: out of time, out of sync, over and over again, dreamlike. The journey was made into a series of events happening, not in clock time, but in road time. This wilderness – this extreme of nature – was leading me to explore my own extremes. It had become a journey to get lost in, to wander, to travel without aim, until sooner or later I would be forced to give it a purpose.

'Hey man! You wanna hear another joke?'

On these long bus rides I always ended up in the front cabin, 'riding shotgun' beside the driver.

'*Another* joke?' The last one he'd told had been a silent two hours ago.

'It was the middle of the night,' he started without any further encouragement; 'this guy was on a long drive through the South when he realizes that he doesn't even know what road he's on. He's lost. And he hasn't got a map. Then he notices a farm set back from the road, so he pulls over his car and walks up towards the house. A big dog starts barking. So, needless to say, this guy starts getting a little anxious 'cos he's a stranger and likely as not there's a rifle aimed at him right at this moment. Anyway, he gets up to the front door and knocks.

'"Round the back," he hears a man's voice call to him. Now, as the stranger rounds the corner of the house, he sees something really weird. In the moonlight, under an apple tree, is a farmer cradling a pig in his arms and struggling to lift this pig up to an apple that's hanging from a branch above him. The pig eats the apple and then the farmer heaves the pig up even higher to reach a particularly juicy one . . . heh, heh.'

The driver laughed to himself, savouring his story.

'The stranger's so surprised by this that he almost forgets to ask for directions; he just stands there watching for another minute 'cos the way the farmer's feeding this pig is driving him nuts.

'So, the stranger says, "Why don't you just pick some apples, or shake a few down . . . ?"

'"Why's that?" says the farmer, while he lifts the pig even higher to get at another apple.

'"Well, it would be a damn sight easier for a start. And it would save a lot of time."

'Now the farmer looks at this guy as if he's said something really stupid. "But a pig don't need no time."'

# 1

There was a cataclysmic lurch and a phenomenal roar of pure, surging force as I farted and flung back the cocoon of bedding. I put the phone back on the hook and padded across the nylon shag-pile to the bathroom where a strip of paper across the lavatory seat advised me that everything in sight had been 'sanified for your comfort and protection'. I de-sanified it. While I rinsed the lenses of my glasses under the warm tap, the face in the mirror returned a wince that might have begun life as a smile. I squeezed a small spot that had appeared overnight, raked my hair with my fingers, had a shower and searched carefully through the layers of clothes and books in my suitcase to find a clean shirt. There wasn't one, so I put yesterday's on again. With an uncanny sense of direction I found my way to the picture window and drew aside the curtains with a grotesque floral motif on them.

'Mmm, perfect day for a picnic.'

Outside the sky was as dim and unreal as the recently elected Reagan. Fine rain blew against the pane and in the street below cars had their lights on. The aluminium-framed mirror glass of the First Chemical Bank reflected identical office blocks. On top, a digital clock alternated time with temperature. 11·45. 84°F.

Through a gap between the tall buildings it was just possible to catch sight of a railway yard where Santa Fe and Southern Pacific rolling-stock waited for somewhere to go. I watched the traffic lights changing at the intersection below until I could anticipate each change within a second or two. When the lights had changed from red to green ten times, I noticed the clock again. 11·50. 84°F.

'Morning has broken,' I sang to myself. 'And the day is in a splint.'

There was no point in rushing headlong into a day like this. The weather and poor sleep had combined to help me start the day feeling sour and glum. I checked the tour itinerary:

DAY OFF. NO SHOW TODAY.
DEP. 14·00. DRIVE TO DENVER. 1050 MILES.

Some day off. I had to start moving if I was to have something to eat and collect my laundry.

Downstairs at least half of our lot were in the coffee shop.

'Morning,' I said to no one in particular.

I sat at a table near the others and waited to order. Elsewhere a few businessmen were dotted about, as neat as cemetery lawns and as upright as columns of printed figures, every last one of them with a nervous haircut and one of those foolish and prissy moustaches that lay beneath his nose like a slumbering rodent.

From our tables floated a series of low moans and fragments of conversation, punctuated now and then by the clatter of cutlery dropped from lifeless fingers.

'Yeow'd screw a fuckin' snake if sumone 'eld its head down for yeow. Yeow've gorra be careful these fuckin' days y'know. Not thar I care. I've got to get a neow fuckin' sout-fuckin'-case 'cos o' yeow, y' bastard,' said Magnet to the truck driver.

He was called Magnet because he had such an unattractive personality. Not only did he have the thickest of Brummie accents but when he occasionally found it 'una-fuckin'-void-able' to use a word of more than one syllable it was his peculiar talent to incorporate his customary flow of foul language.

The rest of the crew – Ernie, Flakey, Vomit and the Colonel – had become so heartily sick of his bragging about how 'inde-fuckin'-structible' his Samsonite suitcase was that the day before they'd held him tight between them while the truck driver carefully placed the case in the middle of the parking lot and slowly backed the articulated lorry, full of sound and lighting gear, right over it. They solemnly handed him the pieces.

I was feeling knackered. After getting back to the hotel from the previous night's gig, I'd spent a couple of hours in the bar, babbling into the mike of someone's cassette recorder – mainly with the intention of impressing his girlfriend. Most of the night I'd lain in bed reading, kept awake by the yowls, yelps and whinnies from the room next door, until the noise had eventually died away along with their supplies of booze and nonsense powder. The shrieking of these men and women in an airless room, so determined to Have a Good Time, struck me as both melancholy and savage. How I wished I had the power to enchant them even further. Imagine the maid's disbelief as she lets herself into the room and finds it filled with these sleeping beauties.

There, my spell would have frozen a woman who stands ready to swallow another drink, but has been stopped. Perma-nently. Around her are others held in place by the invisible strings of an unseen puppet-master. Lifeless and comical they hang, in mid-conversation and in mid-yawn, with not a flicker of an expression on their far-away faces and with their last movement made into a mask . . .

'Hey! It's self-service you know.'

The voice woke me from my daydream. One of the crew was pointing over at the buffet lunch that'd been sitting in the middle of the coffee shop all the time. The Colonel nodded, and smiled hesitantly – with good reason. A few days earlier the upper plate of his false teeth had been broken in a bar-room punch-up. Because we were continually on the move he'd had no opportunity to see a dentist and so he'd had to repair the teeth himself. Unhappily, even the most potent epoxy resin wasn't immune to the warmth and moisture of the mouth and, inevitably, glue-fatigue occurred. The poor Colonel would crack a smile, only to have it crack back at him as his teeth collapsed into a crazy, angular expression which caused great mirth in onlookers. The pieces rattled like castanets as he tried to protest. At soundchecks I often noticed the teeth wedged between two robust items of equipment, waiting for a fresh application of glue to set.

I poked through a mound of baked potatoes that smelt like old encyclopedias while a native beside me – a mound of soft flesh enveloped in seersucker and nylon jersey – heaped his plate high enough for three.

'Sling us over some bleedin' Daniels!' shouted the Colonel.

'What?'

'More Daniels. More Daniel bleedin' Boones.'

I took him over some spoons.

The Colonel was the newest recruit to the road crew. He had arrived from somewhere in the Middle East – no one had found out from where, or why – to find asylum in a life on the road. Because of this, and because he had curly black hair, and because it was his job to stick down all the loose leads on the stage, the rest of the crew had contrived to call him 'Colonel Gadaffatape'. This had since been shortened.

'Try and behave like creatures that walk on their hind legs,' said our Manager.

I hadn't seen him come in. He pounced on someone.

'What's this! Salad! Real men eat raw meat for breakfast,' he said through clenched teeth, only half-joking. 'Anyway, listen,' he continued, 'the generator on the bus is being fixed so we're not leaving 'til late. 5·30 in the lobby. We've kept the rooms on.'

Back in my room I switched on the TV and clicked around the channels.

Click.

'– as soon as they invent it we rent it.'

Click.

A cartoon was on. It had dubbed laughter. Non-existent characters played to an equally non-existent audience. Best left to each other.

Click.

A game show. A man dressed as a turnip was trying to guess the price of a chainsaw. Oh God, they even had this one back home. I hoped he'd guess wrong and they'd use the saw on him.

Click.

'– the earth is a planet in just one of ten thousand million solar systems in our galaxy, the Milky Way. And the Milky Way is just one of a thousand million other galaxies.'

Hmm, this looked interesting.

'Now, what I wanna know is: Who counted th –'

Click.

Click.

Click.

Three bizarre evangelists titillated and whipped up an audience of blue rinses with fake feats of strength. Dressed in leopardskin leotards, they crashed through balsa wood beams and then staggered to their feet. Then one of them was handcuffed. But he couldn't break free.

'I'm gonna give it just one more shot. I don't think I can do it, but I'm gonna try.'

His accomplices waved giant Bibles around their heads as he struggled and writhed.

'Help him! Help him!' they screamed. 'Pray for him!'

It was more than bizarre. It was obscene. I couldn't take my eyes off it. Then suddenly he was free. There was a geriatric gasp of awe, and the wild men talked about the power of something they called 'Lerv'. And they talked a little about money. And then they talked a little more about money. So I watched the millionaire prophets preying on the emotions of the feeble-minded with their shabby tricks and their sentimental promises and their dire threats, while they sold entry into a phoney paradise and advised us to watch the skies for the arrival of a White-Bearded Old Thunderer and his retinue of gassy invertebrates, who would come floating through the clouds on a bed sheet to save us.

There are many things worse than humanity without religion. This was one of them: religion without any humanity.

Click.

Click.

Click.

A soap opera. A cop show. Another soap. It was possible to fritter away three separate hours of television in one hour of viewing by (click) punching the channel changer until all three blended (click) into a single circus of tension (click), hysteria and rotten (click) characterization, with a plot that was no less imbecilic and dialogue that was no less (click) cretinous than if they had been viewed independently.

Click.

A grinning mannequin rolled out a red carpet of insincerity

and read jokes from an autocue. The compère had a fixed smile on his routinely handsome face. When he turned to speak to one of his guests the expression didn't alter, since really he was smiling not at them but at himself. Unidentifiable people fawned over each other: sweaty men with foolish hairpieces, ageing gargoyles with latex faces that had been repeatedly lifted, and babbling starlets who'd powdered their noses on the inside too. The most insecure laughed loudest at the other guests' jokes. Each seemed, pathetically, to need the exaggerated applause that followed each bit of froth. They seemed to expect it. Why? Just because their made-up faces and personalities were part of the electronic wallpaper? Celebrities! What did any of these turkeys have that was worth celebrating? Their self-delusion? Where on earth did they get these people from? I'd heard it said that the TV networks bred these chat show guests in disused sound stages in Hollywood. But there were maniacs too that would do literally anything to be famous, to be on TV. With any luck, one of these would burst into the studio and shoot the rest of 'em.

Click click click click click click.

The movie channel offered a highly emotive domestic drama, a tragic and brutal love story and a star-studded thriller of murder and intrigue: I'd seen them already, whatever they were called this time.

In the event of real drama there was a brochure, *How to Survive a Hotel Fire*, on top of the TV. Rule 9 advised against jumping out of the window. We were on the twenty-third floor. I crossed out the word *Fire* on the front cover.

Now what should I do? I almost laughed. Not for the first time was I forced to recall the episode of *Hancock's Half-Hour* that found him alone in his Earls Court bedsit.

I opened the week-old *Melody Maker*. Here, in an interview, a young witch in corsets and eye make-up was treating us to her views on suicide, heaven and mini-skirts: 'I don't believe in heaven at all. The only heaven I know is delirium. I don't believe I'm going to be whisked off to a perfect place when I'm dead and I confess my sins. I don't believe you come to any Pearly Gates.'

According to the paper, there was a seismic eruption of new talent happening in Britain – an uprising while we were away crusading. There were hungry bands on the loose looking for scalps. There was a nihilistic little combo from Sheffield, the Puff Adders, who thrashed themselves to death in a forty-minute atonal guitar frenzy while telling us our time was short. And a bunch of Teutonic wallies who made music by taking a Bosch powerdrill to a dustbin. I silently invited them to close the lid on themselves. The nearest any of them came to an eruption was the outbreak of acne on the severe-looking youth who played lead hedgetrimmer.

I picked up a novel, *The Third Policeman*, and put it down again. I was enjoying that story so I decided to save it for the bus.

From my travelling bag I pulled out notepads and cassettes and more books. I opened *The Legacy of the American Indian*: 'everything the power of the world does is done in a circle. The sun comes forth and goes down again in a circle. The moon does the same, and both are round. Even the seasons form a great circle in their changing and always come back again to where they were. The life of a man is a circle from childhood to childhood, and so it is in everything where the power moves.'

The view through the window of what used to be Indian land and was now irretrievably urbanized Sunbelt stood in direct opposition to that. Another black glass box was NOW LEASING. In the Sunbelt, cities were growing up and spreading fast. The happy hunting ground had been paved over for a set-square city made from building blocks and bathroom tiles. The monuments of over-achievement stored more data about things than there were things that actually happened. They formed mind-deadening corridors of sea-green, silver, and the colour of raw liver, blocking out the sun, reverberating the traffic noise, and towering over boutiques that only the wives of deposed Filipino presidents would feel comfortable in.

I opened my sketch pad and leafed through the pencil drawings though nothing new had been done since the Australian leg of the tour. There was:

- a left hand resting on a table top
- a chair
- a TV
- a gloomy self-portrait
- more left hands
- a potted plant
- a childish landscape with a farmhouse and a duckpond
- a drawing of a crumpled-up piece of paper.

Some postcards fell from the back of the sketch pad. I could write a postcard home? I found the right one: *Paris through a Window* by Chagall. The man in the foreground had one white and one blue face. (At the time I had on my blue one.) A cat with a human head sat on the window-ledge. Outside a train ran along upside-down in mid-air. A couple floated head-to-head, horizontally. A man in a white suit descended gently from the sky (no doubt surviving a hotel fire). No, I'd phone. Later. Tomorrow.

'What the blues is, the Blues cures,' so they say. I found a B B King tape and put it on. For a minute or two there was the simple sorrow of minor chords, then the guitar took off with a powerful flurry of ringing, stinging, singing notes that hung in the air like steel arrows, followed by a flight of fragile whispers and delights, with needle-point precision they glided . . . At least they did in most of the reviews I'd ever read.

It had long been an ambition of mine to hold a cocktail party and invite several Blues singers. Imagine it: 'Howling, this is Lightning; Lightning, can I introduce you to Screaming. Screaming, meet Muddy. Muddy, Howling.'

I had to go out. I needed to collect my laundry before it got left behind. I picked up my coat and swung it around me in a dashing flourish. The Man in the Iron Mac.

Outside in the corridor a few of the road crabs were having a competition with paper planes. The road crew were called 'road crabs' as a result of a game that had sprung up amongst us in which we made 'ab' the last syllable of certain words. For instance, a cheeseburger and french fries became 'a cheesebab and french frabs'. It was easy enough to follow, as long as you weren't the bewildered barman who was met by Magnet's request for 'a large fuckin' vab and slablab fuckin' tab'.

In the latest game the contestants had to throw paper planes made from dollar bills. Whoever threw the furthest collected all the others as his prize. The start line was the wheel of the drinks trolley, loaded with empty wine and champagne bottles that had recently been jettisoned from the Drummer's room. I took a dollar from my pocket, joined in, and won five. Just then the lift stopped on our floor so I took the opportunity to escape with my profit.

In the lift I was greeted by the glutton I'd stood next to in the coffee shop. Being friendly was his profession. He was full of sales rep *bonhomie*. I thought I heard him introduce himself as:

'Turd Newbank. Glad to know ya. Say, are you with the band?'

'Er, actually no. I'm here for a gynaecologists' convention.'

'Huh?'

'Well, I spend a lot of my time dealing with – '

He interrupted and wittered on, backed by a stretched and fluttering tape of a vibraphone arrangement of 'Spanish Flea'. Long after we'd reached the lobby he was still telling me about his girlfriend. And his weekend home. And his bloody 'Bee Em'. Until mercifully he left.

'Wait 'til I tell my girlfriend about this, she won't believe it. So long now, keep ya powder dry.'

I watched him as he waddled off in his Reeboks. He couldn't have been more than twenty-five.

'What's the difference between a BMW and a hedgehog?' I muttered after him.

As the weatherman on the television had said, there was a 'high percentage likelihood of continual precipitation'. Yes, it was raining. I gazed out through the dotted pattern on the glass door at the front of the hotel and the warm drizzle grazed my face as I walked out. Though the atmosphere was tense and dark and it needed a storm to clear it, the air was soft and humid. Almost drugged . . .

. . . When I looked up, I noticed an unusual shop on the opposite side of the street. Unlike the others it didn't have a garish sign shouting its name and business and, instead of cold blue neon, a warm light glowed inside. I crossed the street without looking either way for traffic. There was nothing displayed in the window. Puzzled, I went inside.

It took my breath away. I didn't know where to look, where to start. On one wall there hung three hand-stitched, patch-work quilts that were in such wonderful condition they might've been newly made. There were tin toys and Shaker furniture, and on the wall in front of me, a '57 Strat, in mint condition too. A card slotted between the strings said 'Fifty bucks'. I ran my hand along a long shelf of records, reading through the titles on the edge of their sleeves. The entire Atlantic, Chess and Motown catalogues were for sale, still in their original cellophane wrappings, and for the same price. And there was more –

'Can I help you?'

She startled me. I hadn't even seen the woman behind the counter come in. Instantly I was taken aback by the way she looked at me, so directly and with such penetration that I was made to feel acutely self-conscious. Though subtle, it was a look of such intensity that for a moment I felt as if I were enfolded in some kind of magnetic or electrical field. I found it hard to take and almost turned away. But though it was uncomfortable, I was fascinated by the experience of her look-ing straight into me, and the knowledge that I was neither a stranger, nor strange, to her. She seemed to know me very well and besides amusement her expression showed sympathy. Yet behind it there was a suggestion of such unbroken calmness and self-possession that I found myself smiling.

The woman was dressed like – well, maybe, it would be better to say that I had the feeling that she might be in disguise, or rather that she could be anything I might imagine her to be. It would be easier to say what she wasn't. It was impossible to tell her age within twenty years; she reminded me faintly of my grandmother because, although there was a twinkle in her eye, I could see that she was not a woman to be messed around.

I spoke at last. 'I was just looking really,' I said. 'It seemed like an interesting shop,' I added casually, while I returned to wondering how much of the stuff I could cram on to the bus.

The woman turned away and went at once towards a back room, indicating that I should follow her. As I did, I couldn't help but notice the way she carried herself. There was something pleasant, almost satisfying, about her movements – youthful and steady, but full of suppleness. She seemed to glide, making no effort beyond what was essential. There was quality in her bearing: her walk, like her gestures, flowed together in unison with something I could only guess at. The only thing clumsy about it would be any attempt to describe it. Better to say that nothing about her gave any hint of imitation.

But what a disappointment the other room was. There were no rare electric guitars, only a carved flute and an old mandolin. The place was crammed, but not with any valuable quilts or beaded hangings, nor any old necklaces or leather cases, nor any boxes hand-painted with delicate flowers. There were no buckles or bangles or silver. A large cabinet had shelves crowded with carved figures and crystalline rocks and china ornaments too ornate to be beautiful or valuable. There was an hour-glass, a small broken globe of the world and a jumble of dolls in costume. A child would have made a treasure house of it but my precious-jaded view saw only something forlorn and unsettling in all the untidiness.

The light made me feel peculiar. It came from an oil lamp that was suspended from the centre of the ceiling by three chains joined to a brass hook. Wherever the light fell it changed all the insignificant objects, so that even the smallest

# BRUCE THOMAS

spaces between them became infinite expanses because of the depth of the shadow that was cast. Yet the whole place had a spontaneity about it, as if it were set up for something, as if it hadn't been here any time at all. But it was also obvious that it must have taken years, decades, to collect so much junk, so many old documents and papers.

I trembled at the amount of material that was in here, because none of it, she told me, belonged to what she called 'the bits and pieces of ordinary human knowledge'. There were no car maintenance manuals, no rainfall statistics, no history of the Bolshevik movement. Indeed, there were few familiar titles of recent writing, apart from one or two books on the new science of quantum physics. As if I might be interested, the woman pointed out a little-known work by the German writer Herman Hesse. She remarked that it was evidently an early work because the writer had still found it necessary to add an introductory note to the effect that 'all fairy stories affirm the identical nature of the psyche of people in all nations, at all times'.

As if to confirm the remark, on the same shelf was a collection of the Greek myths and some old books whose gold lettering had faded on their leather bindings, making their titles impossible to read.

'They look interesting,' I said, pointing to the older books, my curiosity and the fact that they might be worth something allowing me to make contact at last.

'To be able to understand any of that kind of writing you must first have had something of the experience that prompted it,' she said clearly. She noted the reaction on my face, but didn't add anything.

She reached up for a small book which she then handed to

*18*

me. 'This is the best book I can give you at the moment,' she laughed. 'If you use it.'

I opened the book to find it full, or rather empty, with blank white pages but paid her the few dollars she asked for it, becoming embarrassed when I realized that the bills were still folded into little paper planes. I pocketed the book and grinned a thank-you. Without altering her expression, she smiled back at me.

It was only then, when I turned, that I noticed on the wall behind me there hung a series of lithographs showing New Orleans carnival floats in 1906. The theme that year was Utopia: one float was titled, 'Where Castles in the Air are Real'. A red sticker on it said NOT FOR SALE . . .

. . . When I realized that I'd been standing in a daze in front of the hotel for over a full minute, I began walking. There was no Magic Pawnshop opposite: only a big sign:

TIRE & MUFFLER SHOP. HAVE A NICE DAY.

At that moment, the corporate buildings somehow had a new power to oppress and they might have been gigantic sheets of board propped up from behind like a movie set. The light had already begun to thicken and the rain was driving a funny kind of smell up through the drains. Skirting a construction site was a long hoarding where the graffiti vandals had made their sad gestures of individuality with less dignity than dogs spraying their piss over lamp-posts. People in a bus queue coughed, and stood as if their bodies were something they hated having to carry around with them. A bus came and passed by, full, its occupants a swim of faces and unrelated features, separated from my own reflected image by a sheet of wet glass. No one looked at anyone else.

I found the cleaners and collected my clothes. This was one of the luxuries that I really enjoyed: having clean shirts for two weeks, lightly starched and folded with bits of cardboard in their collars, each one sealed in cellophane ready to be dropped straight into a suitcase. It was not a simple luxury: we stayed in expensive hotels, but the expenses we were allowed on the road didn't run to affording their laundry and cleaning services along with everything else (like phone calls, bar bills and food). So I had to go off and find somewhere else. Life on the road was full of these silly contradictions.

We travelled thousands of miles between Holiday Inns that were exactly the same, to see some of the world's most famous sights only from a window across the city. At other times we stayed in places I wish I'd never seen. Or I slept through some of the most spectacular scenery in the world, not because I wasn't interested but because I was bloody knackered. When there was a chance, I'd go out and walk. I spent entire days walking miles and miles of streets, only to get back to the hotel to be taken the few hundred yards to the theatre in a chauffeured limo. After the show there'd be hundreds of excited people milling around, trying to get to see one of us for one reason or another. An hour later you'd be back at the hotel, in the bar drinking, or in your room alone. (Or not, if you could keep up with the endlessly complicated sham of remembering who to lie to about what happened where, and when; ultimately everything became even more blurred, because every lie had first to be told to yourself. There was of course the one exception who didn't lie; but no one had ever met him.)

Leaving the surge behind me, I walked away from downtown and into streets with shops that sold cheap furniture or cheap luggage. There were tacky gift shops and a tacky lunch-eonette. A man with matted hair and three layers of coats shuffled past, taking his lunch from a bottle in a brown paper bag. Bottles in a shop window with contents that had long since dried up, were abandoned and left undisturbed because they weren't worth stealing. An old record shop had a sign that said OPEN in the door. Someone had put it up years ago, but hadn't taken it down – as if the place had gone bust in the middle of the afternoon. No more rocking.

Pasted across a window, a poster proclaimed JESUS IS ALIVE. Across it had been scrawled one word: WHERE? The notice I'd seen in the dry cleaners answered it ironically.

INVISIBLE MENDING – YOU WON'T BELIEVE IT 'TIL YOU DON'T SEE IT.

Here and there I passed empty lots between buildings. There were mattresses and the remains of chickens in poly-styrene cartons. Weeds found a way through chunks of old foundation concrete and scraps of metal sheet and wire. In the railway yard, the rolling-stock rusted in tracks with the years growing between them. No more rolling.

Somewhere far away a radio blared, distorted, another ironic answer. Before it was turned down I heard snatches of Chuck Berry describing in song what I might once have seen around me: cars, hamburgers, rock'n'roll music itself. Just the way it was. I thought it odd that this music and this voice was passing invisibly through walls, and through me, as radio waves. WHERE? indeed.

Walking the streets I looked at my feet and brooded. Next year this area would be full of shops selling toys and candies covered in hearts. Above me, where the rusty fire escapes dangled over the shopfronts, were rooms awaiting occupation by candle makers and weavers: where it would take a two-hour walk to find a tube of toothpaste.

I kicked discarded wrappings under the wheels of cars and was about to kick a screwed-up ball of paper when I noticed that it was a letter someone had thrown away. I picked it up: it was half-written, half-printed, in a childish hand. Each paragraph was numbered.

(1) Your letters don't take long to get to me. I am just very slow in responding because I am so miserable.

(2) I never mention work in my letters because I quit the Park Service. I am now finally working half time in the State's Progress and Analysis Department. The Park Service people were very pleasant but the job they gave me was horenndus. I had to straighten out a file that had been in disoray for 7 years! and they did not give any instructions and I don't want to talk about it. The State job is better – I file all the legislative bills and I am two doors down from the governers. I never thought that me who always dresses in rags would like dressing up because it is not a casual dressing place but I do and I feel a little less worthless.

(3) The problems I've had with jobs, applications, resumes, interviews, employment, and future is the second worst trouble since next to the Krishnamurti one.

(4) I think the best thing you (Liz) and me (Tom) could do is help each other with our futures: what do we want to do in the future, get prepared and all that.

(5) Have you heard from John Ashton? Dad says he's planning to go to Afghanistan in March. I wish I could go with him in spite of the danger.

(6) I would like to be a writer or have my own

business – I have *Entrepreneur* magazine that has tons of suggestions. You and me should maybe start our own business. I had thought of buying this old run-down building and try to make an inside orchard with tropical fruit. Mom's friend Margie Lava (do you know her) a few years ago started a computer database company and now she has over 100 employees and an office in Amsterdam and one off the coast of Mexico. The only friend I had in Santa Fe was going to with a companion buy some old office buildings and he said I could be maintainance man. Would you be interested in starting a business with me? I was thinking about some art form that changed color with temperature or some growing crystal that changed shape, color, and form. I have hundreds of other ideas.

(7) I'll be willing to test my mental retainment next to yours. Let's do some games in that Creative Games book.

(8) The vocabulary words you sent me – most I know and all I've heard of. In 12th grade I was in a class where we had to memorize fancy words and I used a method that worked real good and got high scores. You've probably heard of the method but when you get back we can both try it.

(9) As I read more of your letters, I see some good writing.

(10) You don't have harpoon scars, do you? You were slim and looked good a couple of years ago and I'm sure I can help you knock tonnage off. I have a million suggestions for weight loss.

And there was I thinking that life on the road was taking me away from reality. I didn't want a million suggestions either, just one peak that would lift me out of this cloudy and brooding atmosphere.

Then someone handed me a leaflet.

BREAK THAT $00,000 A YEAR BARRIER!
ARE YOU EARNING WHAT YOU'RE WORTH?
CALL FOR THE MOST EXCITING OPPORTUNITY OF
YOUR LIFE
UK EUROPE JAPAN AUSTRALIA USA
FULL- OR PART-TIME

When I'd walked so far that I was lost and had no idea where I was, or how to get back to the hotel, I found my way back to the busier streets and managed to get a cab.

I got in and told the driver, 'Terminal Hotel.'

As we pulled away, the driver craned his head to the right and introduced himself out of the corner of his mouth. Then, without any further preamble, he told me that he had once driven Frank Sinatra. He waited for me to be impressed.

'Yeah. Really! But not in this cab, of course,' he continued without my encouragement. 'Ya see I use ta drive for a limo company . . . Well, as a matter of fact I only drove him around for one morning.'

'Mmm.'

'Yeah. Would you believe it! He had me replaced because I sneezed in the goddamn car.'

'Why's that,' I said, 'because he's a hypochondriac?'

'Nah. Because he's a dick-head.'

As we approached the hotel he spoke again. 'I remember when the Terminal Hotel used ta have four attendants in white jackets ta work the elevators. The place was so immaculate you coulda eaten your dinner off the floor in the lobby.'

The thought amused me that only the night before the Drummer had *left* his dinner on the floor in the lobby. I recalled it lying there like a pointillist painting. This was but one flourish in a bender of epic proportions. The previous week he'd decided to limit himself to three drinks a day; yesterday, the three drinks he'd limited himself to were Pernod, vodka and bourbon. An earlier episode of this adventure in alcohol left him with the romantic notion of sleeping out in the grounds of the hotel we were staying in. The following morning the automatic lawn sprinklers had been on for a full five minutes before he'd come round. He appeared in the coffee shop, soaked and shrivelled.

Back in my room, I suddenly realized it was already time to leave. I'd no idea I'd been out for so long. I put the clothes in my case and the book in my bag and – the man in the dressing-table mirror caught me by surprise. He was about the same age as me, maybe a bit older, clean-shaven and with his hair cut short and uncombed. Though his clothes were fashionable (somewhere), he was carelessly dressed and in colours that were too pale, or rather not bold enough, for him. There was something weary and undecided about his expression that was at odds with his actual features, so that he looked at once intelligent and sad. He gave me that peculiar smile, which I found almost unpleasant. The mirror was one of those in three sections. I leaned forward until my face was nearer his and then folded the two sides in as far as they would go behind my head. There were lots of him in there: left and right profiles, face to face, back to back, stretching away in paired and prismatic perspective.

No one else was in the lobby. I looked at my watch and it was, of course, Happy Hour. I put my bags down and went off to the bar. It brought to mind the joke about the pub on the moon. (It went out of business: no atmosphere.) This was perhaps the twenty-seventh bar I'd seen on the tour that'd been done out as 'The Captain's Cabin'. Fibreglass was made to look like wood, plastic to look like metal. Everything was made to look like something else: even the load of old rope wasn't rope. It was all as ersatz as the 'Victorian' pubs in Milton Keynes, with their leaded-glass jukeboxes. Neither the creation of an empire in Texas nor the collapse of one in Britain had brought about any flowering of good taste.

The Singer sat between his headphones and behind a book. Miles Davis streamed in through each ear and Jerry Lee Lewis through each eyeball. Or was it the other way round? His gin and tonic was placed next to a bottle of Perrier. The Drummer, already as pissed as a parrot, had, as a bet with the Keyboard Player, lined up along the bar as many different coloured drinks as they could think of: blue curaçao; green chartreuse; a tequila with orange juice made crimson with grenadine; another drink, cloudy-yellow with Pernod; a vodka gimlet, green with lime; a strawberry daiquiri. It was an international exotica of excess. At the far end of the bar a middle-aged couple watched uneasily. She was two stone underweight and wore so much make-up that it probably had to be hauled to her face by block and tackle. A bright red stripe signalled where the vodkatini and processed olive was about to be sluiced over bridgework that was still being paid for. Her husband was decked out in a visual cacophony of checks, with a tie as wide as a tent flap. They were the kind of Americans, with flesh like chicken wings and minds like wet pretzels, who thought that

'natural' was a flavour of yoghurt. It was at the point of no
return through the deadly journey of cocktails that the Drummer spotted them and homed in. The Drummer himself still
wore the same silver jacket that had been stained and wrinkled
by spilt drinks and adventures past – a coat of many curries.
He reminded me of Lord Nelson in Trafalgar Square – long,
thin and covered in shit; although according to him he wasn't
that tall and compared to the size of his genitals, he was in fact
quite short. His complexion had taken on a kind of reptilian
glaze and the couple were cringing behind false smiles, their
heads turned to one side to avoid the full withering blast of his
drink-charged breath, or as we called it, the Dragonsbreath.
The mood began to get distinctly darker as the man was
harangued into an arm-wrestling contest.

'Hansh acrossh the warder,' said the Drummer.

The woman muttered something about intelligence.

'Intelligensh!' retorted the Drummer. 'Intelligensh ish what
gets you out of a shipwreck ... Robinshon Crushoe ...
macarooned on an island full of coconuts.' Then he was seized by
the impulse to demonstrate to them the visual aspects of the
famous British sense of humour. He removed the lower half of
the man's admittedly awful tie with two or three inept slashes of
his Swiss Army penknife, cutting his own fingers in the process
and bleeding on to the man's shirt. An argument broke out. The
Drummer did the proper thing and offered to make good the
damage by drinking champagne from the woman's shoe, which
he had by now removed. The nearest beer was commandeered
but most of it had gone down his jacket before he realized that the
shoe he was pouring it into was open-toed. It was only after
several twenty-dollar bills had been handed over from the tour
manager's float that the couple were appeased.

When I returned to the lobby I found that it had filled up.
According to the ID badges that half the crowd was wearing,
there was an 'Attitude Adjustment' seminar about to take place.
No doubt the participants would be parting with a month's
wages to buy a weekend of being beaten to a psychic pulp by
some hustler. It turned out that there'd been a mix-up in their
booking with the Postal Workers' Disco and Dance. Both
groups milled about excitedly, unable simply to wait for their
rooms to be sorted out. They babbled and bubbled, gibbered
and jabbered, spluttered and stuttered in alphabetical disorder,
managing to be everywhere except inside their own skins.
Small talk switched effortlessly from subject to subject as each
bit of aimless chatter or each bit of self-help psycho-prattle
suggested another. The more trivial the topic, the more dram-
atically and the more emphatically it was spoken about. Empty
eyed, they almost attacked each other with conversation.
Wearily excited, hurried and bored, they spoke nervously, as if
they were afraid of what they would discover if they were
quiet. As if something dreadful would happen to them if they
ever shut the fuck up.

When the crowd did clear, I saw the Singer over on the
other side of the lobby with another person who was pretend-
ing not to be a journalist. The Singer had been observing the
same crowd that I had. I noticed that he'd jotted a few words
in his notebook. No doubt these 'metaphysical jerks' would be
appearing in a song soon. 'Then what do you do to get away
from music?' the writer asked the Singer.

'Don't want to get away from it,' came the curt reply.

The Manager arrived to intervene. 'No thank you. We don't
do interviews. Could you leave please?'

'No, this is public domain. I'm just standing here as a

member of the public like anyone else, just observing my experiences. If he just happens to be part of it – '

The Manager's hands came up as high as his chest and hovered there as he manfully resisted the impulse to poke the offending scribe in the chest with his knuckles. He paused, strained, at that turn-off from the freeway that said: LAST EXIT BEFORE RANT. He shuffled urgently from foot to foot and finally let go of all he was holding back in a volatile flood of insults and threats of legal redress and worse.

'Maybe I should write about you inst – '

'No thank you. Good day. I've no desire to be famous, thank you. I've seen what fame does to people. I just want to be rich, thank you – rich and unknown.'

'Then you'd stand a better chance if you hadn't changed your name to Johnny St Tropez, wouldn't you, Malcolm?' he said as he turned on his heels and fled.

I thanked my lucky stars that I had no intention of ever writing anything about our Manager. Could I stand it, waiting, breathless, for the knock that comes in the night? But there were some silly sods who were intimidated by this carefully cultivated belligerence. One journalist back home, a tall and anorexic stick-insect in a leather suit with a rip in the crutch that kept revealing a renegade bollock, came to interview us over dinner in Sheffield. To prepare himself for the ordeal he'd downed just the one too many. He spent the whole meal hanging on to a bread roll while he buttered the back of his hand.

A youth with a feeble moustache and acne spotted me. 'Hey, how's it goin'? Great show last night.'

'Thanks.'

'Can y'all sign these for me?' He was hugging a brown paper grocery sack full of records.

'Sure.'

'Who're y'alls favourite band?' he asked while I was signing the records.

I trotted out a ready-made answer about liking anything that taps the feet, strokes the thighs, moves the heart, and makes me think.

'Yeah, but what about the King's New Clothes' album, man? That a great cut, isn't it – "Love Lies between these Lips?"'

King's New Clothes' double-bluff didn't work: their name was totally apt. They were a group of little merit and no substance. The music was derivative, technically precise and just contrived enough to make it neurotic. Trying to be tough, it was just as sentimental as popular music has always been. Any so-called creativity was merely variation on routine, blandly decorated with all the necessary fashionable quirks. The production polished all this to a mirrored sheen, so removing any last trace of shade or colour that might have escaped. They sounded just like a hundred, a thousand, others: dull and sterile.

'Yes, they're great,' I replied.

'And how was it recording in Nashville, with Buddy Sheriff producing an' all?' he continued while he opened a book with our photograph in it for me to sign as well. 'No, no, use this felt-tip on the photographs.'

'It's a funny thing,' I said, 'but ol' Buddy must've been pretty scared of us or something, because all the time we were in the studio he carried a gun on him.'

My new friend's expression showed that he didn't find anything odd at all in that.

'I suppose it was in case the music got too wild, in case we played any dangerous chords,' I volunteered.

*30*

Nashville was one place I had felt scared: we'd played there at Vanderbilt University. During the day, before the show, we'd been out shopping. There's a good guitar shop on Broadway and Ernest Tubb's record store and a shop that kits out country singers in kitsch. You might think that Nashville is a holier city than Mecca with so many of the shops run as religious charities, until you discover that this makes them exempt from taxes. We had sat in a bar which sold only Budweiser: a straight dollar for a can which you had to open for yourself and drink from. The day before, the lead singer in the bar's resident band had been shot. Dead. Because he didn't know a particular Hank Williams song.

In our perverse quest for obscurity we'd cut a record in Nashville. It was a novelty for them too. Usually it was musicians and producers called Snake and Pig and Crittur who ran a closed-shop there that kept them all in business.

('Ah jes' don't know how you gert such a great sound on that fiddle o' yers, Pig.'

'Well hog tie me to a 'gator tail and nail it to an ol' blue barn, it ain't nothing but you fiddlin' with those knobs on that ther' board o' yers that makes it sound so good Possum.')

We had a couple of these characters sit in on our sessions to try to give us that authentic hokey sound, except nobody played like that any more. All the records they played on sounded like Martini ads. Pig and Possum were reeling out yards of music at triple the union pay scale. They drove home in chuck wagons that said Mercedes Benz on the front.

'Maybe I should change my name to Dingo,' I mused out loud.

'Huh? Hey! You just signed that Dingo Starr.'

It was an impressively thick, leather-bound book of

*31*

autographed photos the boy had given me. I turned the pages as he spoke. Somehow one of our band photos had found its way in there amongst all the scrawled 'Best Wishes and Good Luck'. This guy still wanted my signature, even though I played second fiddle in an orchestra of four.

'What do you do?' I said.

'I'm a messenger at the Bureau of Fair Trading,' he said. 'It's very prestigious to work there, you know. A lot of rich people work there. It's very respected. Not everyone can get a job there. You have to know somebody.'

Why does everybody in America want to be somebody or, if not, to know somebody?

'I don't suppose I'll ever be in libraries, or on records like you,' he went on, 'or on movies or TV. So it's kinda nice to be able to stand out from the crowd, y'know, and be remembered. I've been in the newspapers a few times with this book, y'see. I check the papers to see what celebrities are coming to town an' then one day, looky here, here's my name in the papers too. I'm not happy all the time at the Bureau of Fair Trading, so I've got this project, y'know, meeting celebrities and collecting autographs.'

Familiar faces, and not so familiar ones, appeared as I turned.

'That's why I collect these. I've shared a few moments with all of these people – '

'But there's got to be more to life than collecting autographs,' I prompted.

'Oh, sure. I mean if I can leave something creative like this behind, something that I've done, I dunno, maybe it'll be important to somebody someday.'

This was making me feel more and more uncomfortable.

Celebrities are made to feel important because of the attentions of their fans. The fans feel important because occasionally they get an autograph or a minute from their idols. So the perpetual-motion machine of vanity is allowed to keep turning in mutual self-satisfaction.

'Er, we've got to go now,' I said, handing him back his book of treasures.

'Oh sure. Thank you for your time. You must be very busy, I know. But something I've always wanted to ask . . .'

There was always one guy, every day, who thought he was the first and the only person who'd ever asked me these questions. He asked them now, giving no time for an answer and expecting none. It was more in the nature of a litany.

'When did y'all start the tour? . . .

Where y'all been so far? . . .

Where y'all go to next? . . .

I mean, what's it like on the road? . . .

I mean, what's it like being a rock star an' all? . . .

Hey man, is this the first band you've been in? . . .

I mean, has anything weird ever happened to you? . . .'

Then, gradually something begins to register.

'Does it kinda get you down, people always coming up to an' asking you dumb questions?'

'Doa't wander off, we're goig dow. . . in a bidit,' interrupted the tour manager with the dodgy sinuses. It remained only for him to settle the bill and sort out the tricky matter of what had happened at four o'clock this morning when the Keyboard Player had returned from his nocturnal prowling: he'd turned the key that opened the motorized gates of the hotel's underground parking lot and as they slid back he had driven the rented Cadillac inside. Once in, he saw that every space was

taken and began to reverse out. At that exact moment the
gates began to close. He was half-way back out when the gates
slammed shut against the side of the car, denting it just enough
for it to need two new doors while the electric motor that
worked the gates burned out and the gates jammed. The car
was freed some hours later.

An awful sound began to pour into the lobby. I poked my
head around the door of the ballroom where the Postal
Workers were collected and stamping. A trio on the stage at
the far end battled through 'All Night Long', playing with a
cavalier disregard for rhythm despite the heavy heavy heavy
heavy on-beat from the drum machine. They swung like the
*Queen Mary* in a sea of Mars Bars. Men in plaid trousers
pranced around women with dresses that billowed. Their arms
hailed invisible taxis, opened invisible bottles of wine, or
greeted invisible friends off planes. Below the waist they
moved as if they stood in wet fish. The tour manager had crept
up behind me. He tapped me on the shoulder.

'Now is the winter of our discotheque,' I said.

'Get tod de bus, dow,' he said, but I knew he was going off
to haul in stragglers from Happy Hour.

I wandered off to buy a paper to see if the review meant
we'd be coming back in another six months. A girl barged into
me and walked on, unconcerned, no doubt held entranced by
the New Age, baby food music that was seeping from her headphones.

I looked over the bestsellers – a rack of novels read by
people on the beach when nobody wants to play volley-ball.
On the magazine stand I scanned and abandoned various
glossies. One was full of the scandals of the celebrated. Fashion
magazines skirted the issues. Here was a magazine for people

who liked to shoot things, with an ad for a gold-plated designer automatic. Others were full of naked women and exaggerated claims for the charms of inflatable rubber lovers blown up out of all proportion. Instinctively I turned to the centre spread – aptly named. A fully-inflated woman lay back and smiled alluringly at me.

The little head began to think for the big one.

But what was this? *Format: The new monthly of art and artists.* Here? In Texas of all places. Maybe there were new tax concessions on art, as well as religion. I opened the magazine at a feature: 'New Artists, New York'.

'Neither abstract, nor figurative. Like romantic landscape in earthquake. Neither liquid nor solid,' gushed the writer of the article. 'The power is not so much in the paintings as in the artist's holding together of all the elements long enough for them to reach the canvas.'

Oh dear. The artist had nothing to communicate but his own confusion and the dismal thinking that lies at the root of all our troubles in the first place. The paintings shown were all just as bleak and worthless as the endless portrayals of happy farmers and happy miners and happy steelworkers that I'd seen on display in the museum in East Berlin. This stuff was just plain bizarre. Freakishness and negativity passed themselves off as originality and style.

'Russell Cronenberg's paintings again raise the censorship question, and while addressing themselves to the controversy that they create, behind all the stomach-churning nastiness, the exploding heads, the rabid growths and the afterbirth eating – is there a serious artistic vision?'

'No there fucking isn't!' I shouted.

People tried not to stare.

# 2

_Where y'all go to next? . . ._

Driving at the legal speed we wouldn't have reached Colorado
inside a day. So the driver had a standing instruction to keep
his boot down, on the understanding that all fines and bribes
to traffic cops would be taken care of. It was the only practical
way to travel, bearing in mind that a loaded Silver Eagle doing
ninety takes nearly a mile to come to a halt.

We bought the bus and kept it based in America. Unlike the
standard bus, ours had been completely refitted inside so that
it resembled a scaled-down version of the Royal train. It had
three rooms, each with a set of stereo and video equipment. In
the middle room there was even an electric piano. There were
bunks, a toilet, fridges, cupboards full of sweaty suits, and a
microwave. Every fitting was detailed with the kind of fussy,
mock-Spanish embellishments that passed for elegance in that
neck of the woods.

I'd already had an argument with the Keyboard Player over
who was having which bunk in the back section. There were
four bunks: upper right and left, and lower right and left. The
lower bunks were simply sofas. The upper two folded down
from the roof on large hinges and were held in place with steel
bolts. These bolts were of course permanently mislaid or lost,
so the upper bunks would sway and bang around. The whole
room was carpeted in phoney Eastern rugs with fringes and
tassles so that it both looked and sounded like the proverbial

knocking-shop. On a long trip, or after a long night, this room would be full of slumbering, sweating people sprawled, supine, in varying degrees of catatonia. For this reason the back room was called Jonestown.

I sat with the others in the middle section of the bus. Nobody would nod off until we'd made a stop for essential supplies. Opposite me, the Singer looked sourly over the top of his glasses. Tsss tsss tsss tsss tsss – a horrible, grating rattle came from the earphones he was wearing. Not loud. Just quiet enough to be really irritating. (I promised myself that the next time a Japanese tourist asked me for directions I'd send him the wrong way as revenge for the Sony Walkman.) The Singer's forehead was leaking sweat which ran into two fierce, vertical creases in between his eyebrows. I recognized in his face the precocious and intelligent child who was better at kicking around an idea than a football. He would have become easily annoyed at being given new games that were quickly learnt, and if they didn't go the way he wanted an accident would've been contrived to send the pieces scattering from the board. Now he was writing in a black notebook, which he did almost continually. Whether he was exorcizing his thoughts, or whether his thoughts were exercising themselves at his expense, was impossible to tell.

The Keyboard Player's daughter had once caught me lost in thought.

'Do you know how your brain works?' she asked secretly.

I looked puzzled and considered how I could best explain about neurones and associations of memory and all the rest of it. But before I could formulate my condescension she continued:

'It's like your head's full of little ants. They work together like a little ant farm. When you think, a little ant thinks the thought for you.'

'You know,' I said, 'it *is* a bit like that.'

'You see! A little ant just thought that for you. They never stop.'

Today the Keyboard Player himself was wearing a T-shirt, which bore the message KILL 'EM ALL AND LET GOD SORT IT OUT. He did things like this only to wind us all up. Sometimes it worked very well. He was given to changes of mood that were so quick and dramatic that we'd given him not one but several nicknames. The miserable 'Reginald' (Maudlin) and the noisy 'Lionel' (Blair) were just two of many.

The Singer on the other hand had an accent that was given to wild variations, particularly during stage announcements. In Liverpool it became a thick, nasal Scouse. It was a top o' the morning, may the road rise to meet you, bejabbers brogue in Dublin. In London it became a Cheltenham cockney that recalled the early Jagger. It was important only to remember what town you were actually in. The Singer might well have been called Curt Reply, but we simply called him 'The Pod' owing to an increasing tendency to resemble the shape of those creatures from *Invasion of the Body Snatchers*.

Once, we'd drafted the scenario of a film we thought we'd soon be rich and famous enough to make. In this proposed film the Keyboard Player had been cast as a teenage electronics wizard whose pent-up emotions had one day compelled him to flush his parents' pet poodle down the lavatory. The Drummer was to have been a declining soap star with a bottle in each hand and a floozy on each arm. The Singer would have been working for a clandestine and enigmatic agency that dealt with computer data and surveillance. While I became an advertising executive who hated his job and ran off to Cornwall to listen to Bulgarian folk music whenever things became too much to bear.

At an earlier time we had simply been the Crow (of kitsch), the Buzzard (of the beat), the Macaw (of the macabre) and the Owl (of art).

The traffic lanes were still filled up with workers going home so we took the opportunity to make an early stop for essential supplies and pulled off the road into a vast parking lot. We filed out singly towards a giant supermarket. A Ranchero pick-up swung in a large arc across the parking lot and came to a halt in front of the entrance. I noticed a bumper sticker: A SMITH & WESSON BEATS 4 ACES. This certainly wasn't SAVE THE WHALE country. Two cowboys got out. They weren't the yee-haw, country and western festival kind of cowboy, reeking of aftershave and with neat studded shirts. These were morose cowboys in Duck Head overalls whose boots were covered in cow shit. When they spotted us you could feel them wishing that we were each holding a hand of four aces.

The supermarket was a grid of aisles – a small city with no traffic and no weather. I wandered in right-angles between oversized and identical pumpkins, frozen lasagne and dog biscuits as I followed a smoothie who was stocking his cart with provisions for a romantic evening: one avocado, a pack of frozen prawns, thousand island dressing, two filets mignons, frozen peas, then two candles, a packet of paper napkins and a bottle of Californian champagne. I was surprised he didn't throw in a packet of condoms. By now a couple of bottles of full-bodied red had found their way into my own trolley.

There was a wait at the check-out while a woman cashed a

pile of special-offer coupons cut from a newspaper. The cow-boys were in front of me, their trolley loaded down with six-packs.

'They're going to distill it down to a pint of real beer,' I said, pointing out their trolley to the Drummer who had just wheeled up behind me.

The cowboys gave me a look. I wished I hadn't spoken. The Drummer's cart though was loaded for serious bevvying: two litres of blue-label Smirnoff; a quart of tomato juice; a bottle of Wurr-sester-shier sauce, bought at a prohibitive price from the import-deli counter; jars of onion salt; celery salt and ground black pepper; fresh lemons and tabasco. Bloody Mary! The Keyboard Player arrived and added an extra bottle of vodka to the cart just to be on the safe side.

The girl on the check-out zipped her light pen across the barred price code that was printed on each item. It occurred to me that it wouldn't be long before credit cards were as obsolete as cash. Soon we'd all have identifying lines tattooed on us at birth, which could be read off in supermarkets along with our purchases. All the details would go to a central information processor and our bank balances would be adjusted accord-ingly. (There is even a town in France where a system like this has been tried as an experiment – all transactions entailing only the exchange of digital information.)

'It won't be long before we've got lines tattooed on our arses, like the mark of the beast,' I said to no one, but loud enough so that everyone could hear. 'We'll just sit up on the counter and be zapped with the light pen straight through to Amex.' I wished I hadn't said that either.

The way out of town was through a wasteland of housing developments and shopping malls. Fast-food franchises stood, as if propped together from sheets of plasterboard, like big playing-card houses: Wendy's, Big Boy, Long John Silver's Seafood and the improbably named Carlos Murphy's. We passed through the sprawling, middle-class suburbs with twee, rustic-sounding names like Hollyleaf Village and Wake Robin Rise. These were planned communities with illuminated jogging tracks. Barely finished, there were piles of piping left here and mounds of sand there. Treasure Island was a few neat bungalows on a low mound that had been bulldozed into place. The caterpillar tracks still showed where the red mud had been squelched down and the grass hadn't yet grown. Further along was another development fronted by a row of perfectly vacuumed lawns with discreet security-company signs: ARMED RESPONSE.

Life was dangerous out here: ten yards came between the air-conditioning of the house and the air-conditioning of the car parked in the drive. Fresh air was where you played golf. Otherwise, the open air was for the poor in the inner city where fat, elderly women with swollen feet and asthma lived with silent partners with tired hearts, and where drawn and worn-out mothers with their untidy parcels of kids tried to make their homes amongst the statistics and the steel.

We rattled metallic over a railway bridge. The flanking girders flickered rhythmically as we crossed a wide, wide stretch of thick water. Then we were sucked on to the Beltway and out past carpet-sample warehouses, whose windows were filled with giant day-glo prices all ending in 99c. Someone had stopped illegally to strip parts from a car that'd broken down. A jet was coming in low for the airport.

On leaving any mid-American city the view would be much the same: the K-Marts, Safeways, the fast-food huts, warehousing, housing developments – hardly distinguishable from each other. It was this, more than anything, that made touring America seem so endlessly repetitive. But unlike the tall buildings downtown, here things were built horizontally to line the highway for a few more tacky miles.

For the first travellers who crossed America, it took a hard year and a harder half year on top of that. In this bus it would take a handful of days. By plane, it took a handful of hours and you'd be able to see the same TV shows and the same burger bars when you arrived on the other side. But why get romantic about it? New ground can be broken only once.

An hour passed. Miles passed. But not nearly enough. The terrible twins were in bed with their bottles. The Singer removed his headphones and looked over the top of one of the British papers he'd tracked down this morning.

'Sometimes I think the soul of man is like a troubled sea –'

'What!'

'Prince Charles,' he said, and finished reading the paragraph that reported a speech given by the Prince at a naval-officers' dinner. The Singer's tone of voice left me in no doubt as to what he thought about it.

'He's quoting Jung though, isn't he?' I said uncertainly.

'Well, yeah, I know that.' He didn't know either.

There was tension here. A gently mocking tone had crept into his voice, opposed by my just-too-polite disregard of it. This conversation had to stop. Floating over me, like a speech bubble in a cartoon strip, was a bubble waiting to burst open with ideas; and if it did, the Singer's multiple-warhead, bullshit-seeking missiles would be launched to bring them down in flames in a second.

A funny image presented itself to me: on a bus were four

card players sitting around a table. They had been there for five years. One played poker. One played bridge. Another played rummy.

The cards were dealt out and each player took his turn to throw down a card. One declared a full house. The other trumped it. 'That's thirty points to me,' the next announced. One missed a turn.

And sometimes we would play together.

It occurred to me that all the tension and distancing of the day was the only state from which we could move closer together when we had to play for two or three hours every night. We were at once contending powers and cooperative forces. The tension had as much to do with balance as it did with conflict. For instance, how much more in touch could a good rhythm section be? Intimate one minute, tough the next: the Drummer and I had to agree instinctively where the beat was. No agreement meant no rhythm.

I looked out of the window. We were still driving through no man's land. I sighed.

The Singer reminded me that only recently I had remarked that a bored person is a boring person. Every few minutes one of us took his turn to mutter the current tour catch-phrase: 'What a horrible state we're in'. The horrible state was still Texas.

The Singer switched on the radio.

'And here are the local news headlines: There will be no school bus tomorrow. Mrs Fritz, who reported that her parrot fell off his perch today, says that the bird isn't seriously hurt but is still quite stunned.'

I began rummaging through a box of videos and held up *Dr Strangelove*. But how could we watch that again? We could by now recite the entire dialogue in unison. The Singer read from the back of another video left by a heavy metal group we'd once rented the bus to.

'It is the year 2015 and savage gangs roam the streets. To combat them it takes a special kind of cop, half-robot and –'

'Half biscuit,' I groaned.

We put the video on anyway. The warrior hero, a robotized man, could transform himself like a Japanese toy as the plot required. He had an armoury of replaceable head modules that made him a kind of hi-tech Worzel Gummidge.

'Armageddon outta here,' I said.

I made my way up to the very front of the bus and into the driver's cabin. Here, like an Andy Warhol movie showing a fly sitting on a man's nose for eight hours, another film was shown regularly. Similarly minimalist, it showed a road.

A hundred more miles passed, straight, out of my life until suddenly the road unwound like a microphone lead and dropped gently through washed-out gullies and hills into a broad plain. The look of the place amazed me. The dull, aching emptiness could barely be held by the eyes. To photograph it would need a 360° lens. It would also make colour film redundant. The edges of the windscreen alone put any kind of border on it and diminished the huge, arching sky with nothing under it but the road. This place was half-way between anywhere, going or returning.

Away from the strip of highway, the telegraph poles and the road signs riddled with bullet holes, the place looked exactly as it must've done before the Yoorpeens ever came. We passed miles of potato fields and a cluster of mobile homes with duck-boarded ramps – silver caravans, Airstream trailers that looked like thermos flasks that had turned inside-out and spewed out old

*44*

fridges, some car seats, a length of clothes-line and a basketball hoop. The lives inside stretched only as far as the flex on the curling tongs. Only little lives could be lived in so much space. We passed a solitary motel with a single string of fairy lights; I pictured pink divorcees sitting with fat men who drank beer from cans and wondered where all the years had gone.

I felt as if we were driving past the wrecked dreams of solid homesteads. These should have been homes all self-sufficient with milk from cows and bread from the fields. These were meant to be houses built with bare hands from the stones and trees gathered from the land where golden women in gingham aprons baked chocolate-chip cookies. Instead someone inside watched a rerun of The Waltons and ate another Twinkie.

The space mocked any instinct to settle and made everything in this town with no centre look flimsy and feeble and temporary. This was the outer limit of a huge, unwieldy and fragmented way of life. These were the last echoes of the blood-red noise and the juddering neon, the lurch and flow of acrylic suits and all-night cynicism, and the lack of vision in the glazed eyes of squealing showgirls and wrinkled golfers that calls itself civilization.

For a while we followed a truck with beautiful chrome tanks. The back of the tank reflected our elliptical image back at us, like a photograph taken through a fish-eye lens. Later we followed a jeep. It had the customary bumper sticker: IN THE EVENT OF THE RAPTURE, THIS VEHICLE WILL BE DRIVERLESS. Eventually the jeep turned on to a dirt road that ran up to a weathered grey house, doubtless stocked to the rafters with freeze-dried sweetcorn and tear-gas grenades. On the beds would be pillowcases with little eye-holes cut out of them. Even the surrounding grain silos were aimed at the Commies.

I turned on the radio: 'God sees all and remembers.'

An amazing-grace voice, shot through with thunderbolts, sermonized and screamed Biblical text. It wasn't Sunday.

'Jesus wants to know how many haven't sent in their five dollars for the home worship kit. A small price to be saved.'

'Yes. He is risen,' another voice declaimed as if it were speaking of some awesome loaf of bread. The sermon was sliced with ads for a savings and loan company. Religion and money were as inseparable as, well, as money and religion. Jesus saves and Moses invests.

On another station a crusty and benign old uncle patronized some children with a childish song, '– if I could put time in a bottle'.

Further along the waves we joined a taped interview with the sax player of Big Thing. Without being able to see the pleasing personality which he imagined he was presenting, the radio revealed a tone of voice which had dubious charm. He trotted out one cliché after another: 'best food and best hotels . . . we couldn't do it if we didn't like it . . . just like one long party . . . rock'n'roll gypsies . . .'

Apparently Big Thing have just shot a video on the streets of Chicago, causing such a commotion that the police had to swoop in and close down the set. With mock innocence the interviewer wonders how the word had got out. The sax player declares his own surprise with just enough calculated smugness so that we know that he was the smart operator who called KRAP to get the rumour started.

The interviewer thanks him for his time.

'Yeah, nice to meet, I mean *talk* to you,' replies the musician.

A track from their album fades up. Their music, anthemic and larger-than-life, is too grand to get inside of anything.

The CB radio channel was more interesting – they were definitely trying to get inside something. I listened to the voices of truck drivers. The older ones were all trying to sound like John Wayne, the younger ones like Sylvester Stallone.

'Huh, ah, er, we be a, er, horny buffaloes lookin' fer some sweet pussy.'

I snatched up the hand mike. 'Hi y'all. We be a stagecoach full of English, middle-class faggots. Hello cowboys!'

I recorded their reactions on my cassette player and played them back again over the CB. Then I taped the angry replies and so on, until I was sure I had one guy arguing with himself.

My glee was cut short when something in me recognized that I talked and argued with myself all the time, in much the same way, and without any special provocation.

Why hadn't I turned this dynamo of ideas into generating a huge income which would allow me to retire? I considered writing a pot-boiler with lots of juicy bits in it. I began sketching out the plot of *The Walkman Mystery*, a series of grisly killings in which the victims are all found strangled by the headphone-lead of their own personal-stereo system. I took the notebook from my coat pocket and began to outline my hero, a quixotic loner, the world's first bass-playing detective:

*He lived in an apartment in a mental block, haunted by the ghost of an idea, a guitar-string puppet with a suitcase history. The detective walked the streets looking for clues . . .*

When the cheques had started rolling in I'd nail an electric guitar to the mast of a yacht, and sail off in search of a palm-fringed island where the natives would look at the guitar and ask, 'What's that?' That would be the place I'd stay.

Then inside the notebook I found a pound note. It must've been there for weeks. I began to analyse the characters of the Queen and the Chief Cashier through their signatures. On the reverse side Sir Isaac Newton gazed out, his telescope and prism lying flat and two-dimensional against some algebraic equation which included the absolute and inescapable $t$ of time. It is the same letter $t$ that begins the words *tour* and *tedious* and *Texas*.

The road made a long turn and headed north by north west. The world behind the glass looked as flat and phoney as a Hitchcock back-projection. The deep swell of the land met a skullcap of foul sky in a long dark edge.

Out of the nearside window I looked at the trucks we overtook, their drivers staring ahead in some private trance of their own. It was like watching a funeral procession going by in reverse. Once in a while one of them would glance across quickly and then look away with a vague expression suggesting that he hadn't really been interested in the first place. All of us were thinking now only of where we wanted to be; we'd all had enough of where we were.

I thumbed through the pages of the tour itinerary to read, again, the list of cities we still had to visit. Like a government fiddling the unemployment figures, I tried different ways of looking at them that would reduce them or make them seem smaller by comparison. I had dozens of these itineraries at home; just reading one of them could give you jet lag. On the inside page was a message from the Management: 'America is a very big place and consequently a modicum of pacing would be appreciated. This isn't a rehearsal. God does not allow one several throws at the coconut.'

I was less worried about throws at the coconut than I was about being stuck on the Big Wheel.

I had, by now, finished reading Flann O'Brien's *The Third Policeman*. At the end of the book, it becomes clear that the main character has been dead throughout the story and that all the funny incidents and all the queer, ghastly things that have been happening to him, are happening in some kind of hell he's entered as a consequence of a murder he's committed. Just as we begin to realize that he's dead, he manages to find his way home to the house he used to live in with the man who'd been his accomplice in the killing. Although our murderer thinks he has been away a couple of days, his accomplice is twenty years older and dies of fright when he sees the other – the ghost – standing in the doorway. The two of them quit the house together and begin again the cycle of the same funny and terrible events, yet the murderer is just as surprised and frightened at everything as he was the first time it happened, as if he'd never been through it before. It is made clear that this kind of thing can go on forever. 'Hell goes round and round,' says the author in his epilogue. 'In its shape it is circular, and by its nature it is interminable, repetitive and very nearly unbearable.'

This was the band's third time round the world in three years. Round and round and round the world we had gone until it had all blurred together. I watched a Sony in Sweden, had a sauna in Australia, met a Buddhist in Scotland and saw a Holiday Inn in Egypt. There was yoga in France, nouvelle cuisine in Nigeria and the Lucy Show in Tokyo. The same records and the same clothes could be bought in Shepherds Bush and Manhattan, in Singapore and Rio. In every main street I'd ever walked down I had kicked a red can down the gutter: the world had been Coca-Colonized.

I looked down the list until I reached Los Angeles, the last stop, three weeks away. I actually found myself looking forward to that town where life appears to revolve, like a Big Zero (no less), around the car wash, the mirror and the waterbed. Meanwhile we went through towns like Birdbrain, Cheeseburg and Pentecost. I began to see myself spending the rest of my life sitting, and eventually dying, on a sodding bus, like some clapped-out country singer. Dying on this bus was the last thing I wanted to do! I was about to curse everything when I realized there was no need to. I had a bad case of touritis – the blue disease; the traditional so-called remedies are all well-known. In effect they amounted to an invitation to throw myself on to a fire in order to avoid drowning. It seemed especially ironic that I should feel like this considering the number of sneering pop songs that had been written about ordinary life and its supposed miseries.

Of course it wasn't always like this. There were times when it all made sense. After all, nobody plays a piece of music just to get to the last note. There were some nights when everything went with that effortless kind of swing that requires a certain kind of effort to allow. Nights like those were never the same and could not be repeated; they contained a feeling of being a spectator as well as a participant. They were almost joyous though the feeling wasn't a simple affirmation; this joy was far more complicated: a lot of the new songs were tales of manipulation and laddered tights.

I delved into my bag and found the catalogues of bicycle components and read them again, hoping there might be something I'd missed. The next few minutes passed in reconsidering the gear ratios and frame angles of my proposed new bike and, of course, the most important thing: whether it should be finished in Starmist Black Metallic. That decided again, a certain sense of inner security was restored. Conversely, the cost of this bike would be well into four figures and I would be unable to leave it anywhere, except, perhaps, manacled to the Eiffel Tower. I would have to keep this mythical bike at home as an object to be revered; another one would have to be bought to use.

Next, I fished the newspaper from my bag. The headlines were about the holy war in the Middle East. 'Holy war' is one of those expressions that carries its own in-built contradiction: like 'military intelligence', or 'rock'n'roll hero' for that matter. I made a heartless attempt to plough through the daily casualty list of the disordered spirit. There were the usual reports of killing and corruption, the claiming and the blaming. There were photographs: terrorists with handkerchiefs across their faces hurled bricks and fire, a criminal held a coat over his head, and somewhere behind the anti-radiation mask that made him look like a fly there was a soldier – the disappearing face of humanity. Instead, one came face to face with wheedling and carping, and numbing rhetoric; all it really amounted to was shoddy exploitation and big sticks continuing to turn the history of the world into nothing more than the history of crime.

While half the world starved and hoped only for its next meal, the rest of us were fed shit – lame, casual lies for fools who are not even considered worthy of practised or professional deceit. Moralists moralized. Pessimists pessimized. The truth seemed no longer to be required. Soon, perhaps, it might not even be allowed.

One option remained: to despise or to dread. And I opened one of the bottles of red wine and glugged back a third of it.

*51*

'You're not going to send that one back then?' joked the driver. I liked him because that was all he would say for the next hour. And so I did him the favour of not telling him how I was feeling, as if he didn't know already.

Once the bottle of wine had been emptied into me, all the emotions that were bottled up in me were displaced. The thinking was swamped . . .

. . . I was cycling around in the wilderness. The rain beat down on me so hard that it made me dizzy and I had to stop and sit down on a rock. When my head cleared and I looked up I saw a winged shadow in the form of a man approaching. Then, as my eyes focused, I saw that it was an Indian who wore a feathered head-dress. A fanlike pattern of the finest creases at the corner of each eye came not from exposure to the elements but from a love of laughter.

'Who are you?' I said.

'Hoo Koo E Koo.'

'Who!'

'It sounds like the name of a Taiwanese bicycle factory, eh?' laughed the Indian. 'It's a native word. It means "Indians who live at the base of the sacred mountain".'

'But there isn't any mountain!' I exclaimed, sweeping my arm around me. 'There isn't even any reservation –'

'There are always Indians here,' he interrupted.

'But this is nineteen eight –'

'No,' he stopped me again. 'This is now.'

Then he stepped over to the bicycle that lay beside me and sent the front wheel spinning in its forks and spoke almost reverently.

'There is nothing so huge or unstable that it can't be balanced on a single point, you know, if only this point is at the centre of gravity. Find that!' and then he roared again with a wonderful laugh that echoed around the invisible mountain. 'Find that, and you have found the point of everything!'

Now, he stepped closer to me to whisper some of his native wisdom.

'Remember what you have seen, because everything forgotten returns to the circling winds.' It was, he said, a Navaho saying.

'Oh, you mean: Those who do not remember history are condemned to repeat it,' I said, quoting the more familiar version.

'Yes,' answered the Indian firmly. 'Just as you, who do not remember your *own* history, are condemned to repeat it!'

And all the questions that the boy with the photograph album had asked me reverberated from the unseen peaks as I stared into the spinning wheel . . .

# 3

'How y'doing Ernie?' I said, as I leaned my bike up against a pile of loudspeakers.

'All right mate,' Ernie replied, putting down the guitar he was restringing. 'Fit as a butcher's dog. How's yerself?'

'My left ear's still done in from yesterday,' I said. 'That Pod keeps cranking everything up louder and louder; the treble from his bloody guitar amp is slicing off the top of my head. I wish I was getting paid by the decibel.'

'All right chaps?' said the Drummer, who came in half a minute behind me. His left eye looked red and swollen.

'What you done there, mate?' said Ernie.

'Stripper,' said the Drummer.

'What? Belt you one, did she?'

'No, paint stripper. I'm getting all the paint off the beams in my new gaff. The missus has been on at me to finish it before we go off on tour.'

We were half-way through a week's rehearsal. The following weekend, a gig at the Glastonbury Festival would kick off our ANNUAL WORLD TOUR. Already each day saw us starting a little later. The Singer and the Keyboard Player had yet to arrive and so had half the road crabs who were probably getting in a last round of golf.

'Can you two sign this for a friend of mine?' said Ernie, passing an autograph book to the Drummer. The Drummer signed the book and handed it to me. Under his signature was a motif, a pair of crossed drumsticks, entwined in the message: To Amanda, Passionately Yours.

'I was in the Record Exchange the other day,' Ernie told me as I signed and returned the book; 'I found another album by one of your old bands. Hair down to here!' he laughed.

'Every one a golden memory,' I said.

'Every one a golden shower,' muttered the Drummer.

I picked up the plastic toy that he had left on top of my amp the day before for me. It was a severed finger that hopped about when wound up. I made the appropriate gesture with it.

'Do we want to run through anything on our own?' he asked.

The Drummer had made up a cassette of all the older numbers that we hadn't played for some time and that we would have to relearn. When he switched the player on, instead of the muscular and sensitive noise we expected, we got the Care Bears singing a happy tune about how they were going to care for me and you. It was his young daughter's favourite tape.

'She's always doing that,' he said. 'I should've checked before I came out.'

I told Ernie about another band I'd worked with who had a deafeningly loud guitar player.

'In the end, we took the knobs off his amp, turned the volume right down and then glued the knobs back on showing number three. When he thought he was right up on number ten, he was really only on number seven. It's an old trick but it might just work.'

Ernie gave me a pained look.

I began tinkering about with the Keyboard Player's

synthesizer until I managed to get it to sound like a penguin eating a treacle sandwich. After ten minutes of this I looked up and realized the other two had gone to the pub.

I walked over to the Royal Oak automatically, kicking empty pizza boxes and other discarded wrappings into the gutter and between the wheels of parked cars. An empty bottle lay just behind the back wheel of one of these cars. After a moment's debate with myself I picked it up and put it beside a wire-mesh fence where three lilac flowers I didn't know the name of paid no heed to the mess around them and pushed their way through ice-cream wrappers and crisp bags. Outside the pub two scrawny men sat with a fat woman, looking like Van Gogh's potato eaters, ploughing through bags of crisps. I glanced down at the remains of several screwed-up packets around their feet and gave them a black look which they found easy to ignore.

Inside the pub I found the Keyboard Player, the rest of the road crew and the Drummer, who was telling them about an old mate of his who played country music in a bar band with the unlikely name of the Tex Pistols. This friend had rung the Drummer on the previous evening with an urgent request to step in, as their regular drummer had let them down. The gig was in a Mexican restaurant in the West End. The band had a price list for requests pinned up at the side of the stage. 'Hey Good Lookin'' was at the top at £25. There were others down to a fiver.

'You should've played "North to Alaska",' I joked.

'We did.'

Meanwhile there were two other conversations going on. One concerned an offer of a million dollars that was once made to Harpo Marx to speak even a single word in a film. In the other, Ernie was relating how his father's regiment had tied chameleons to their helmets as a form of camouflage. The end of both stories was swamped by Peter O'Sullevan's climactic commentary on the two-thirty from Royal Ascot.

The Singer came in, still smarting from a review of a recent film in which he had had a role, where all the parts had been taken by various singers and musicians: 'None of the participants in this film has acted before. They don't here.'

Our tour manager had parked his car and followed the Singer in. He handed him a wooden box containing a selection of take-away sushi which had been collected from the Kensington Hilton. The Keyboard Player, who hadn't been watching too closely, asked if he could have the coffee cream. The Singer had begun taking cameo acting roles as a move towards becoming an all-round entertainer. If he kept scoffing sushi at the rate he was, he wouldn't have much longer to wait.

After the rehearsal I cycled home across London avoiding the main roads by cutting illegally across parks, or taking back ways. However I had to join the main road for a stretch. Another cyclist, riding the same kind of expensive bike, passed me going the opposite way. We exchanged a brief smile of recognition. It was the opposite of the frosty expression worn by two ladies who arrive at a garden party wearing identical hats. Our smile was, like the grin exchanged by two men who drive the same classic car, simply to confirm each other's good taste.

Fifty yards further down the road a man getting out of his car swung the door open right into my path. Pride very nearly went before a fall under one of Ealing's dustcarts, as I was swiped and sent skidding by the carelessly opened door.

It had rained all summer. The sun had had the good sense to

stay in California. In London, the sky was a shadeless grey, dark and damp and promising a fall of rain. Seven gulls that had ventured this far inland followed the course of the canal. The noise of planes coming in to land at Heathrow was a precursor of thunder.

I stopped at the crest of a bridge over the canal and watched the constant stream of jets reflected in the ribbon of stagnant water. In a small boatyard, a barge with weeds that grew just above the waterline housed stacks of rusting Dexion. On deck a wicker basket held a foot-square garden of bright begonias, quite naturally the colour that some plastic crates were trying to be. Piled up in their hundreds in the yard were unidentifiable objects fashioned from white fibre-glass, protected by rolls and coils of razor-edged wire in case anyone might discover a use for them. Further along were ten thousand weathered planks. A sign that read NO MOORING might as well have read 'No Business'. Behind these defunct businesses I could see a row of industrial units numbered neatly from one to seven, and behind them there was a calm, cold sea of suburban roof-tops broken only by the icebergs of a gasometer, a church tower and an office block. In the distance a train began to slow from 125 miles an hour so that it wouldn't plough through the buffers at Paddington. I noticed the man fishing. He'd been here in the same spot every day that I'd passed.

'Had any luck?' I shouted.

'Haven't had any of that for years.'

He sat as if held by the dispirited aura of unemployment. His rod dangled a lifeline into the still, dark water as he appeared to wonder what he could possibly pull out of it that would change anything. What made things worse was that he lived in the affluent South East, on the right side of the tracks.

His hands supported his head, his knees supported his hands and the government reluctantly supported the rest of him.

After a few minutes there came a woman with a fat beagle which she kept calling Darling. Across the canal, three dogs in a yard began yapping viciously, as if they were guarding the entrance to the Underworld where the Imortal Powers, a local gang, had sprayed its misspelt graffiti at the entrance to a tunnel.

A man came along the pavement over the bridge. He was searching short sightedly through his spectacles case for something. As he got nearer and then stopped next to me, I saw that his glasses were lying in his hand in three pieces and that the two small screws that attached the side arms to the frame were rolling around in the case not six inches from the end of his nose. I was about to help him when he stopped, squinted up and down at me, and spoke:

'Where d'you get a bike like that?' he asked straight out and then laughed. He was maybe fifty years old, which made him about the same age as the suit he was wearing.

'America,' I said in answer to his question.

'They make bikes like that in America?'

'Well no, I bought it in America but it was actually made in Taiwan.'

'Yeah, I know that,' he said dismissively. 'See, if you told that lot up there in Yorkshire that you can get bikes like that in America, they wouldn't believe you, would they, eh?'

'What lot up in Yorkshire?' I said.

'What they don't realize, see, is that there's a world surplus of coal. See, I know a chappie lives in stockbroker-belt Surrey, drives a Mercedes motor car, lives in a house reputed to be worth a quarter of a million. Well, he's off to America tomorrow – in fact, he might even have gone today – off to America to do a big deal. See. Eh? And there's all them cunts up in Yorkshire, on strike, scratting about in their two-up and two-downs, eh? Hah!'

He laughed and walked off down the other side of the bridge, not looking ahead, but still looking for the loose screws.

On the Saturday the tour party met outside the Shepherds Bush Hilton and we got on our hired bus. As we headed west out of London and on to the M4 I sat in my preferred place, up front beside the driver. We raced a 747 towards Heathrow. I couldn't understand why we weren't gaining on it; it appeared to be hanging motionless in the sky.

Out past the airport half the cows in a field were standing up and half were sitting down, unable to decide whether or not it was going to rain. After a while the driver switched on the radio but because the engine was so loud it cancelled out all the mid-range frequencies leaving only a dull, thudding bass and making a harmonic nonsense of the treble so that there was no tune or words to be heard, only a succession of abstract noises.

Not far past Bath we turned off the motorway and headed south. We were met by one old MG coupé after another, coming the other way in twos and threes, on an owners' club rally or a treasure hunt. The occasional patch of meadow, dotted with buttercups and sometimes ablaze with poppies, stood out because of its rarity; though, as we drove along a high ridge, it was still possible to see some beauty in the country and to picture how it must have been before agribusiness had pulled its green blankets across it all.

We pulled up in front of our hotel in Wells and got out. In

front of us, taking up more than half the street, was another coach.

One lady in a flower-print dress and with a pastel cardigan draped on her shoulders took the arm of her companion with the rows of imitation pearls and elastic bandages around her ankles and helped her to make her careful descent of the three steps to the pavement.

'Did you see where that chappie put the luggage?' said the first anxiously.

'It's all right love. They're taking it up to the rooms.'

'I'm dying for a cup of tea. My mouth thinks my throat's been cut.'

'– as long as it's wet and warm.'

As the receptionist checked us into our rooms I was pleased to note genuine democracy had prevailed. A phone call earlier in the week had ensured that the Singer, the Manager and the tour manager had already reserved the rooms with four-poster beds, which looked out on to the market square and the cathedral.

The cathedral is smaller than it looks. The towers at either side of the façade are squared off, yet somehow the impression of the whole, the proportions, implies spires that aren't there. The building's lines invite you to see something that is only suggested, saying as much by what is left out, like the spaces in a B B King solo.

The hotel was typically English. There were Dralon-covered Chesterfields with tapestry cushions and a fireplace filled with an arrangement of blue silk hydrangeas. On the shelf above were Royal Doulton ornaments of characters from *Wind in the Willows* and on the walls were tinted prints showing pheasant shooting. Parked on the cobbles out back was a line of Saab Turbos, Audi Quattros and GTis.

*61*

Up in my room I switched on the electric kettle and then the television, only to be greeted by a close-up of Martina Navratilova's bobbing bum. I half-watched the tennis final as I unpacked a few things but the picture kept breaking up on important points. When I'd made the tea I turned over to another channel and was lucky enough to catch the end of a documentary about the Taylor brothers of Stockton-on-Tees – three brothers who had been hand-building bicycles the same way for nearly forty years, which were now ordered by customers from around the world. They sat in their workshop, reminiscing for the interviewer, while they toasted bread in front of an old electric fire.

'This American lad sent me a drawing with all the measurements in centimetres and queer things like that,' said one of the brothers in that peculiar local accent.

'Ah doan't believe in proagress. As you get oalder you see that it isn't really proagress at all, it's oanly change, and not always change for the better – you knoa – like giving cannibals knives and forks.'

I went out for a walk: it was more than two hours before we needed to leave for the festival site. Outside I met the Manager who had just bought himself a flagon of 'Kneecracker' scrumpy.

'Are you coiled,' he said tensely, 'ready to rock?'

'I hope not,' I replied. 'We're not on stage for six hours.'

I realized I hadn't eaten anything all day and though I didn't feel hungry I started looking for somewhere. I passed by a café with a broken sign that, looking like a Scrabble hand, read B K RS OVE and went instead to the Friendly Frier. I found a table in the back and ordered cod, peas and chips.

'Codpiece,' shouted the woman to her husband at the frying

range. She pushed the posy of plastic primroses to one side of the table, handed me a knife and fork and turned on the radio in case I wanted to listen to the cricket from Lords. The radio commentary told us that someone had an interestingly placed, square, shortish leg – which clearly accounted for why he'd scored only two runs in the past twenty-six minutes. The dining room at the back had recent coats of yellow and green and white gloss and a childishly painted mural of an Alpine scene was also obviously new. A card on another wall said WE COOK FRESH NOT FROZEN. A new leaf had been turned over. Meanwhile I tried in vain to ignore the thick, musty aroma that had taken root.

Back at the hotel, everyone had begun to assemble for the off. I flicked through a slim booklet, *What's On*. Apart from agricultural and historical events it appeared that *we* were what was on. (I disqualified a barn dance featuring the Lazee River Jazzmen.)

The tour manager came over and handed me twenty quid in cash for daily expenses, a pass that would allow me access to all areas of the festival site, and a meal voucher that would entitle me to a portion of vegetarian lasagne in the backstage catering tent.

As our minibus approached the festival site it appeared that the worst of the mud had begun to dry up but there were still half-acre swamps dotted around, where cars and vans were stranded axle-deep in ooze. As our short line of traffic crawled along behind a tractor, a girl was struggling to get through a hedge. On her face I recognized the mildly distressed look of someone whose trip was going weird. Near the gates a sullen boy held copies of *Socialist Worker* for sale. A headline asked, WHAT WENT WRONG? At least one of the answers was here,

holding copies of *Socialist Worker*. A banner over a tent enig-
matically advertised HOT KNIVES – leaving a gap in the market
for any hot fork or hot spoon salesmen. We got stuck in the
field near the backstage area and a few people came to help. As
the wheels bit into the soft ground again our helpers were
thanked by a shower of flying dirt.

The mobile hut that was our dressing room was conveniently
placed beside the urinals and contained three chairs for our
exclusive use. In the large backstage area dozens of people
wandered about or gathered in small groups. Three generators
thundered out the power for the lighting and sound equipment
on the stage, the stage itself being incorporated into a huge
pyramid made of corrugated sheets.

I ran into the bloke who used to do our publicity, who was
now managing a folk-singer who had played a set earlier in the
day. Unlike us, he was staying down for the three days that the
festival lasted. He pointed out his tent. Above it flew a flag
that read I NEED A BUNK UP.

'I've only had one offer so far,' he said, 'from a fifty-year-
old witch.'

We walked together to one of the small peripheral tents
where the solo and acoustic acts did their sets. On stage was a
rancid ranting autopilot megaphone gobshite alternative com-
edian. His act certainly was an alternative to comedy. As
abrasive as crushed velvet, and like a psychiatric case history
come to life, the poor, witless bastard openly paraded all the
pain and rejection of his life – his wounds undressed and his
disease exposed. Maybe he would die without realizing that
humour can actually heal. No doubt a flock of editors and
producers would be bleating for his signature on a contract at
the end of his set.

*64*

Outside again a few children danced around unselfcon-
sciously or carefully picked buttercups out of a patch of nettles.
Leaning against a Land Rover was an older flower child who
had left his orbit and burnt out years ago. He was so emaciated
that he looked as if he'd been sucked inside out. He'd probably
been arrested more than once just for looking like that. He
called me across and introduced himself, giving his name as
Jefferson Airplane.

'If you can remember the Sixties, then you weren't there,' he
wheezed.

From the side of the stage I watched a few songs from the
group on before us. The stage bounced up and down beneath
me, yet it felt safe enough. The skeleton of the pyramid had
been built from the long trunks of pine trees bolted together.
Thick plywood flooring rested on beams that had been slung
across. It was better that the whole structure did surrender to
the rhythm: anything more rigid might've been shaken to bits
like a bridge brought down by a marching army. It was a
curious sight: laser lighting equipment lashed by ropes to the
inside of this pointed shack.

Daylight had gone and people all over the site lit flares and
torches. Warm, twinkling pools of light stretched away over
the hills transforming the place into a medieval encampment
so that it might've been the set, or the setting, of a historical
epic.

Back at the caravan it was nearly time for us to go on and
the pre-show rituals began. I wondered what to wear. Usually
I got into a rut, particularly if we were having a run of good
gigs so that, like a football manager wearing a lucky suit that
would help take his team all the way to Wembley, I stuck to
the same stage clothes until they began to stick to me. I sat,

almost slumped, in a chair and began nibbling a piece of dry bread for want of something better to do. Before a show I always felt tired, as if I didn't have the energy I knew I was going to need.

The Keyboard Player lit another cigarette and began pacing up and down the caravan like a man in a maternity ward.

The Singer went off to the caravan next door for the first of his three visits to the lavatory. It was always three.

The Drummer rolled up the short sleeves of his T-shirt and tucked them into the shoulders. He pulled another chair opposite the one he sat on, folded a towel over into a thick pad, laid it on the seat and began to loosen up his wrists by drumming on the pad, starting with a hundred shuffle rhythms and progressing through a series of single-stroke rolls and flams and paradiddles and all the other rudiments that only drummers know about.

Someone made the joke about the brown M & Ms. (There is always a contract for each gig made between the manager and the promoter. This contract has what is called a rider – that is, the group can specify its requirements such as minimum stage area, dressing-room facilities, food and drink to be provided and such like, which the promoter agrees to provide. An American group of rolling clones called Aerosmith had a rider which required promoters to provide them with a huge dish of M & Ms. The group had gained a certain puerile notoriety by insisting that every last brown-coloured sweetie was removed. Otherwise, the gig would be off.)

Now, and every minute for the ten minutes before we were due onstage, the tour manager would announce the time. The tour manager had a problem with his sinuses. It was not the sort of affliction that went unnoticed.

'Ted bidits,' he announced.

'Ted bidits,' we chorused back.

Nide bidits came and went. We particularly enjoyed sebed bidits and then no one took any notice until altogether we sounded out the alert for wod bidit. The Singer leapt up for his last visit. The Drummer stood up and with his arms straight out in front of him twirled his sticks so hard that it set up a draught. The Keyboard Player picked up a piece of cheese and then put it down again and lit another cigarette. I changed my jacket and then realized I hadn't any guitar picks.

The door banged open and in barged a man carrying a sheaf of papers and a woman wearing headphones and carrying a mike and a recorder.

'We're from Australian Radio News and we'd like to ask you about Glastonbury.'

As the radio crew jostled through the doorway the woman bashed against a trestle table and sent several open cans of beer tumbling and splashing across the floor.

The Drummer leapt to his feet.

'See! It's never the band that makes the mess, but it's always the band that gets the blame.'

The Manager, who had just returned from the stage, hoisted the first Australian by his lapels out of the caravan.

'We're not interested that you're interested.'

When we got to the side of the stage I was handed my guitar by one of the crew.

'That's right, strap on the posing poles,' said the Manager. The pre-set tape had finished. 'Right, kill and grill. Run on!'

The set began as spiritedly and sloppily as first nights generally do. Half-way through, the Singer began to deviate from the xeroxed list of songs that we each had taped up near us, first adding songs that weren't on the list, and then stretching out one of the songs and gesturing for us to play more and more quietly, putting his arms out behind him and flapping with his hands to silence us.

I stepped over towards the Drummer. 'I see the Albatross is back already.'

We improvised an arrangement trying to sense where to place the next note in much the same way as a tightrope walker places his feet. Then the lighting man missed one of his fades and plunged the stage into a few seconds of blackness, which he'd done often enough already to have earned the nickname the Prince of Darkness.

At the side of the stage, one of the road crew was kept busy changing the Singer's guitars, replacing the two or three strings that were being snapped on every song and changing microphones that had taken too much saliva on board to function properly any more. He had also to keep his eye on the electric kettle so that hot tea with honey and whisky might be shuttled onstage to soothe a throat that was being made raw, as all the tempos were taken just a little too fast and the words spat out like a chainsaw running through a dictionary. The set built towards its tense and thrashing climax.

We played safe with the encores and cruised through old favourites, rabble-rousers and crowd-pleasers, with the lock-tight efficiency that only comes after hundreds of gigs. I had time to nod a 'hello' to a few familiar faces in the front rows of those few fans who followed us just about everywhere. They included the pair of twins – whose names I always got muddled – card-carrying, flag-waving members of the Labour Party who admired the Singer's socialist principles.

Also there was Lorenzo, an American dentist who worked

round the clock in order to spend all the money he earned on hire cars, hotels and plane tickets in following us wherever we went. He had a peculiar intensity about him. He would appear backstage and speak guardedly, like a ventriloquist with an invisible dummy, always ready to note any triviality. He was part of a network of similarly intense young men who followed and catalogued our every move with a detail that went beyond the obsessive. Not only would Lorenzo be making a bootleg recording as we played, to add to the hundred and thirty-five that he already possessed, but he would somehow contrive to get the xeroxed song list that was on top of my amplifier, which would then appear along with every other list of songs from the tour in the quarterly newsletter that they circulated amongst themselves. Members of this secret sect were en-countered in every place, instantly recognizable by the way they spoke casually but were always dying to know who, what, why, where and when. For them, everything was invested with huge significance. One day in Oslo a strange Norwegian might drift up beside you and mutter, 'I hear you go out for lots of walks.'

I'd spoken with Lorenzo many times. He was an intelligent man, yet talking about anything other than the minutiae of the group was, for him, small-talk. He made excuses when we invited him to spend time with us away from where we were working, yet he paid the network fantastic amounts of money for a collector's item such as a record with the label printed in Israeli. It was as if he actually preferred the public image and didn't want to endanger it by brushing against anything more normal.

Over on the other side of the stage were the two from Oxford: the young lad whose father would drive them both all round Europe on a motor-bike to see us. And there was the extraordinary American woman who hitched right across the world. To everywhere that we went by bus or by plane, she would somehow find a lift. We would even see her now and again, standing with a gigantic suitcase at the side of the road in sub-zero temperatures. She managed to appear at every concert in a different encrusted ballgown, long-sleeved gloves and a tiara, wearing them without a hint of kitsch, as if they were second nature to her. She never revealed what the attraction was in following us. Only once did I overhear her saying to someone that she believed we might lead her to what she called 'something special', but that she didn't know what it was.

There were other fans who were sad and silly people. A woman had changed her name to match the names of women in the songs and then sent letters to the Singer: 'I waited, but you never came'. There were men who sent page after page of word-salad poetry which found 'flights of winged alligators carefully measuring the marble with black rubber telescopes'.

Our agent, who had been watching us from the side of the stage, thought the set was a cracker and I agreed that it had had its moments.

'You'd better get to the dressing room or you'll freeze your bollocks off,' he advised.

'No,' I said, 'I don't sweat much. I've got a Drummer to do that for me.'

And indeed I had. After one gig we managed to wring enough sweat out of his T-shirt to fill a pint glass and we got as much again from his jeans. But he soon replenished the lost liquid.

At six in the morning, I was woken by the rattle of scaffolding being erected and, looking out of the window, I saw that market stalls were being set up. Beneath my window a stall was being loaded with garish-coloured nylon blouses and sheepskin slippers. At twenty-past seven somebody began playing Danny Kaye singing 'Inchworm' for a child that wasn't interested in going back to sleep and, while the inchworm was methodically measuring the marigold and telling us that sixteen and sixteen are thirty-two, a fat pigeon came and sat squawking on my window-ledge just to make sure that I didn't get any more sleep either.

I got up. I found I had no toothbrush with me so I squeezed an inchworm of toothpaste on to my finger and rubbed it across my teeth and gums and then went to have a kipper and read the Sunday papers.

The Drummer was still at the bar and looking like he was a few vouchers short of a toaster. He ordered another vodka and tonic.

'Good morrow squire,' I said with mock enthusiasm.

'Don't you start,' he said. 'I've had a trying night.'

# 4

*I mean, what's it like on the road?...*

Dear Chaps,

This is the most complex itinerary that some of you will have encountered. It is however designed with your mind in mind. Unfortunately it is still necessary, even in this upwardly mobile computer-age for you to *read* the damn thing.

Please note: dates may be added on days off.

To avoid being pestered we are never booked into hotels under our own names. As we stand in the hotel lobby waiting for our keys the receptionist begins calling out for: 'Mr Red Snapper; Vince Posh; Norman Wisdom—who's Awesome Wells?'

Once you start making up names the list is endless: Jack Uzi, Norman D. Landing, Gideon Shandy, Hugh Jampton, Ted Bidits, Albert Ross, and on and on.

'Can we get anything to eat?'

'I suppose I could do you a sandwich. 'Ow many wants 'em?'

'But I didn't turn the volume up on stage...eh? What? There's five, six, seven of us.'

'I can do cheese, ham, or cheese and ham.'

'I don't normally ask other girls, but, eh?, I'll have cheese. And what about a drink?'

'T' bar closed at one o'clock. There's a machine on t' sixth floor sells drinks. You'll need three fifty peas. I've got no change.'

'OK, just one toot and then we'll definitely get some sleep. Eh? Don't worry, I've already packed.'

We go to the Rover's Return and, though we can't get a drink, we do see Elsie Tanner and Ken Barlow: we are at the Granada studios in Manchester to mime our latest release. Also on the programme a cerebral and sexless singer from Sheffield is to address a Britain waiting with bated breath on the subject of his vegetarianism. The floor assistant is in an awful flap.

'Nobody told me about the chair, I suppose nobody thought to tell me about the chair, I mean why should I know about the bloody chair. Bloody prima donnas.'

The vegetarian, so I begin to gather, will not appear for his interview unless a certain type of high-backed Georgian chair is furnished for him; now, at the last minute, the floor assistant has to try to get one from the props department.

'Everyone else can talk while they sit on a normal chair, can't they?' the floor assistant says to whoever is listening. 'Or maybe he needs a special chair so that he can talk out of his arse.'

A drummer from a group we once toured with comes to renew our acquaintance after our show at Brighton's Top Rank. I recall, without affection, how, every single night, as we got on the coach after a gig, he would announce, 'Well, lads, it's all down to a fuck, a fight, or a bag of chips.'

He weighs about sixteen and a half stone now.

Backstage after the gig in Liverpool, we've dried off and changed clothes. The tour manager starts letting fans in for autographs.

A Scouser and his mates get their tickets signed in turn. When he gets to the Singer, the Scouse lad asks, 'Have you gorreny nude photies of yer missis, like?'

'No,' replies the Singer uncertainly, knowing he's being set up.

'D'ya want some?'

It's the middle of the night and bells are ringing. I get up and run into the Keyboard Player on the landing. We get hold of a fire extinguisher and prepare to be heroes, but we find that it is just the Drummer, who has short-circuited his bedside teamaker by trying to make mulled wine in it and has somehow triggered off the automatic fire alarm. A voice over the pa asks all the guests to assemble in the lobby until the all-clear can be given. After a few minutes I walk out into Princes Street. At the other side of the street there stands a familiar figure, shivering in his dressing-gown and with a hastily packed suitcase beside him. It is the poet who is our support act on the British leg of the tour. He is crestfallen; he hasn't had time to backcomb his hair into its usual Highway 61 Dylan look.

'Is it safe to go back in yet?' he asks in a Manchester accent that makes the words come out like thick gobs of congealed cream. 'Our family crest was four white feathers on a yellow streak.'

A film crew has followed us to Aberdeen in order to get some documentary footage. Now the director sits alone in the hotel bar. It's late. I slide into the chair next to his. Without turning his head he speaks: 'You see that plastic strip along the front of the bar?' he asks, his voice trembling. 'You see where that gold strip is supposed to join the other one and there's that gap?

That's really annoying me. Things like that make me really angry.'

'Yes,' I agree. 'I sometimes notice things like that.'

He turns his gaze to search my face. 'You know Nick?'

'Yes, I know Nick.'

'He's a strong man.' He looks away again. 'He's a strong man. Isn't he?'

Roger, who is driving our coach around Europe, used to work for a firm that took parties on day trips to the seaside. The highlight of his day came when they were well into the return journey — the passengers had had their singsong, their heads lolled in slumber and everything was quiet. At this point Roger would turn on his microphone and ask matter-of-factly, 'Now, you're all wankers, aren't you?'

While watching his passengers in the rear-view mirror, by applying a few short stabs to the footbrake, he would make them nod in unanimous agreement. That was, until the day one old chap was wide awake and made trouble about it.

'But do you love me?'

The couple must have been deep in private conversation when I'd sat at the table next to theirs. They have been tense and silent for some minutes, but now the girl has spoken.

The man replies. He has a middle-European accent and, thanks to the raincoat he always wears — collar turned up — one could imagine him to be an agent who might now be required to answer, 'Yes, the tulips in Berlin are very pretty at this time of year.'

'But, listen to me,' he says, 'because tomorrow we shall be in

75

exactly the same place, at exactly the same time. I don't want to have to explain it all again.'

'But do you love me?' the girl repeats.

'You will not have to do any more than you have already been asked. I don't want any problems tomorrow, so that is why you must be clear now.'

A minute passes. Beneath their table there is the sound of shuffling. I try to watch them in the reflection of the restaurant window, so that I don't have to look directly over at them.

'I don't want to have to explain it again,' says the man.

There is a moment of scuffling. 'I don't have to speak to you,' says the girl.

And after a minute she asked again: 'But, do you love me?'

It's nearly midnight as I walk along with a bunch of Swedes who are leaving the Concert Hall. I overhear a conversation between two English girls:

'He must've had a lot of relationships.'

'Yes, you can tell by the words.'

'Well, he's an artist, isn't he?'

Hermann the German, the promoter of the gig we are to play in Munich, sends a telex:

Additional information you need, if you haven't already received it.

Our festivals are known for running stickly on time. We want to keep it that way.

I insist that the crews of all bands arrive on the site 3.30 hours prior to the stagetime of their bands

Bands are to arrive at the latest 2 hours prior to showtime.

Leave the hotel on time.

Be aware of traffic jams on the day of the festival.

I will not accept any excuses for arriving too late.

Penalty is 50% of the fee.

Again I insist that everybody is to arrive on time.

Please find enclosed plans showing position of lighting towers, Red Cross area etc.

Please note there are no showers backstage.

Best regards.

I am lying on my bed reading and I don't hear the cliché as it passes my window, but I hear an almighty crash in the car park outside. From my window I see the spread-out carcass of the TV that has just been ejected from the window of the Keyboard Player's room two floors above mine. The electrical circuits of the television are still warm and, as the gentle drizzle spatters it, vapour rises.

I knew it had to happen one day. But no one throws a TV through a window just for a joke or out of tradition. I go up to the Keyboard Player's room. When he opens the door he is still shaking. I don't know what he's mad about yet.

The Mancunian poet (now known to us as Lord Biro) is added to the European leg of the tour. He too thinks it funny that no one will understand a blind word of what he says. At the Plaza in Copenhagen some horseplay results in a picture in his room being smashed. We carefully remove the remaining glass from the frame and replace the picture. Now comes the problem of disposing of the glass. We can't leave it in the waste bin or the damage

77

will be noticed and charged to the room. It has to be dumped. We take the pillowcase from the spare pillow and place the spears of glass inside. That done, the pillowcase has to be abandoned where it won't be found too quickly and where no one will be injured by the contents when it is found. The roof is decided on as the best place, but to be safe the parcel is to have a warning message, though it won't be written in Danish. The wording is debated. Danger? Broken Glass? No. Lord Biro considers for a moment and then savours the words: 'Beware, Shards'.

'Breakfasht ish ready boysh. Boiled eggsh and ham. Ish real good!' Ma Bodie, who runs the small hotel on Prinzengracht, speaks English like all Dutch people do—as if she has a mouth full of Weetabix.

Two minutes later her voice peals through the loudspeakers which she's had installed in every room: 'Come on boysh, breakfasht ish ready.' I totter, bleary-eyed, downstairs. In the breakfast room a small battalion of boiled eggs in steel egg cups is lined up in rank and file on a table next to a plate piled with sliced meat.

'Let's just have a pot of tea,' I say to Ma Bodie; 'I don't like eggs in the morning.'

She brings a pot of tea and then tries to tempt me into having a slice of cooked ham. She picks up a slice and dangles it into her mouth like Cleopatra with a bunch of grapes. 'Mmm, ish *real* good.'

She gets on the intercom again: 'Come on boysh, breakfasht—'

'Fuck off,' a voice echoes back down the stairs.

'Oh, you boysh are so grouchy in the morningsh.'

One of the road crew appears, white faced, and speaks to Mrs

Bodie: 'When the maid tidied my room did she by any chance notice a sort of small, folded-up paper packet on the bedside table, 'cos it's not there now?'

'Why?'

'There was, erm, something I want in it, I mean, written in it, on it.'

A minute later the dustbin is emptied out over the kitchen floor and he is picking his way through the old tea bags and egg shells.

Ma Bodie looks on. 'Musht be a real important phone number.'

I walk along a street of houses in Haarlem and hear a record being played in a basement, a Blues ballad that was recorded decades ago in a basement club in Harlem. I get the feeling that this surely is underground music, that it will never see the light of day.

The Keyboard Player and I are out walking. It's late and we've had a few bottles of *sangría*. He heads off into a multi-storey carpark because he wants a piss. I don't, wait a few minutes, look inside and can't find him. I continue walking.

As I turn into the piazza, I see what look like a dozen gigantic sweetcorn towering against the sky, buttressed by the thighbones of dinosaurs. A concrete Christmas tree above, with a nativity scene, melts and runs down beneath them. Through an arch I see a jumble of granite blocks built in a ridiculous, reverse perspective. I climb over the mesh fence that surrounds this fantastic work and begin to wander and wonder. The Templo Expiatoria de la Sagrada Familia is massive and painstakingly detailed. Decoration and embellishment begin to appear everywhere. It

*79*

reminds me that masons are not just people with funny hand-shakes who run the police force.

The figures of the nativity look down just as they look down on the daily crowds that shuffle into the shopping centres to buy Nikon, Rolex and Sony and then hurry away through the square without once looking up.

An uneasy sensation creeps over me and when I look around I see that several large Alsatians, security dogs, have formed a loose and restless circle around me. Some instinctive intelligence prevents me from running or panicking. It allows me to sit, and so the dogs too begin to settle down. Then soon, after thirty or forty minutes, they go back to where they came from and so, quickly and quietly, do I. Outside in the square again, I look at the church. Nearly a hundred years since building started and two hundred years before it will be finished, I stand there and try to picture how it will look when it is completed—just as its architect Antonio Gaudi did in 1926, a second before he stepped back to be killed by a passing tramcar.

It's night and we're flying over a large city. The Keyboard Player in the seat next to me leans across and looks out of the window.

'I wonder who changes all those light bulbs,' he says.

The NO SMOKING and FASTEN SEAT BELT signs are switched off. The cabin staff begin wheeling trolley loads of arid concoctions of microwaved pap around.

'Would you gentlemen care for dinner this evening?' the stewardess asks us.

'No thanks.'

She moves forward to the next row of seats where the Drummer and the Manager are sitting.

'Would you gentlemen like to eat anything?'

'Yes,' replies the Drummer. 'Pussy.'

Thank you for coming to Japan. I went to your concert and I enjoyed and excited very much. It was been just nice, the hearty singer and classical phrase, I can't tell all. I am very surprised at arrangement. I believed your heavy and melodious very firmly, genial and splendid. Please take care of your health. What a beautiful hair you have. If there are any mistakes in this letter please overlook them. It is my pleasure and I am studying English. Good luck to you.

The record company have taken us all out to a sushi lunch. Even the impeccable politeness of the executives is tested by the tour manager's insistence on speaking Japanese, a language which he has been mastering for over a week. At the end of the meal thanks are exchanged. The tour manager looks in his phrase book:
'Domo arigato.'
The head of RCA Tokyo bows. Unfortunately the tour manager has chosen this exact moment to make his own bow. A doctor is called.

Thirty minutes from Sydney harbour by hydrofoil takes me to the nearby seaside resort of Manly Island. On the front, facing the sea, is, yes! the Manly Paradise Motel. What would it be to stay here, I wonder. My companion loses no time in claiming a sun lounger for her newly discarded clothes and is now on tiptoes on the diving board.
'Perhaps we'll see you later,' I shout from the side.

•

We have an evening off in Sydney, and Chuck Berry and Bo Diddley are playing a concert. I've already seen Bo. He's staying at the same hotel as we are. I went up in the lift with him. He was wearing a crimplene leisure suit, puffing on a pipe and speaking to someone about buying a ranch in Tasmania.

At the gig it is Bo who appears first. He strolls through his hits with his famous rectangular guitar, which is covered in pink fur.

In 'I'm Evil' he's improvising:

> *I'm a crawling king snake.*
> *I'm a hoochie-coochie.*
> *I'm a trouble child.*
> *I'm evil.*
> *My middle name is misery.*
> *I'm a . . .*

Bo mumbles and hits a chord: he's running out of ideas.

> *I'm . . . evil.*
> *I'm a . . .*
> *I'm also very untrustworthy.*

Very untrustworthy! Next he'll be telling us that his library books are overdue.

Chuck Berry is on next, backed as usual by a local band he's picked up in the bargain bin. He whips through his tunes. He's got a suitcase of cash up-front and a plane to catch. In the middle of a song he turns to the Australian guitarist and nods for him to take the solo. The guitarist hits Chuck with all his hottest licks. He puts everything into this guitar solo.

Chuck hangs back from the mike for a bar or two. 'Now take another solo,' he nods again. The guitarist has been suckered. He turns red, tries to pick up the solo, repeats a couple of phrases, then freezes wishing he was anywhere but here. Slowly a grin spreads across Chuck's face. An evil grin.

I spend three hours scouring Adelaide for an Indian restaurant. The sense of anticipation would have been spoilt by simply looking in the Yellow Pages and calling a cab. When I get back to my hotel room a woman's face gazes from my pillow. I approach and look into her unblinking eyes. Her skin is orange and finely textured. Her lips are like those of a fish that floats dead on the surface of a pond. I tenderly lift the head, still in the box that reads: HELLO, I'M MARIE, YOUR EXTASUK COMPANION. I find the bellboy whose pass key the others used to put their sex-shop purchase in my room. Then I take a bottle of ketchup from a room service tray that has been left in the corridor. There is no one in the Singer's room. The bellhop opens the door, I put the head in the lavatory bowl, lash ketchup all around it, close the lid and leave quickly, ahead of the game.

I am going to stay up all night to see the Cup Final transmitted live from Wembley. I'd watched my lot win the semifinal and then on the way home from the game it had slowly dawned on me that I'd be on tour, in Australia, during the Final.

Nobody else is interested in staying up to see the match; I doze and am woken up with an alarm call. Half-asleep, I switch on the TV. Outside the window it's dark, while the room is filled with the electronic light of a blazing Wembley. Half a world and half a day out of sync it's all wrong somehow.

I try to get excited about it, try to feel the way that I feel I should. But it has to be admitted that, from here, I just don't care. Without turning off the TV and without closing my eyes, I go to sleep.

We are driving in from the airport that once rejoiced in the name Idlewild, passing hillside after hillside of cemeteries. Behind them the skyline of Manhattan becomes visible through the afternoon haze; there is a moment when, after staring glumly at the fenced-in car lots and the fenced-in playgrounds and the fenced-in factories that will never re-open, the hazy mood brings on a trick of perspective that confuses foreground and background, so that tombstones and skyscrapers merge into a continuous panorama where subways worm their way through the graves of millions.

I walk from the Guggenheim, through Central Park towards the Met where there are two-storey-high murals by Chagall to see. By the Tavern on the Green there is an old-fashioned carousel where children are queueing to ride. I stand, and watch the blur of faces going round and round and round, wondering why it disturbs me so much.

CBS New York take us on an expense-account dinner. We eat at Joe's Pier 51, a seafood restaurant near the company's offices. The specialty of Joe's Pier is steamed crab claws. On every table in the restaurant there is a pamphlet that tells us the story of the crab and about the House Specialty: 'and so the crabs are not killed. The claws are humanely removed and the crabs are then returned to the sea. However, not much is known of the survival rate of crabs without claws.'

•

# THE BIG WHEEL

Rather than take our bus through the Friday rush hour, we take a cab to the soundcheck for tonight's gig at the Palladium. When we want to get back to the hotel to eat and to change there isn't a cab to be had anywhere. For the week that we're in New York we have hired two cops from the 13th precinct who moonlight as minders. Showing little imagination, we call them Starsky and Hutch. One of them, who still carries his police radio, gets on to headquarters and rustles up two police cars. Three of us get in the first car as passers-by wonder whether we are the most unlikely looking criminals or the most unlikely looking cops they've ever seen. The driver and Starsky begin to bitch about a brothel keeper on their patch who they've been trying to bust for years, and who has just won another acquittal.

'Yeah,' says the driver resignedly, 'but while the mother was in court we went round and superglued all his fuckin' locks.'

Now we sit at some traffic lights near 42nd Street. There is trouble on the corner. Starsky taps the driver and points it out; the car takes off through the red stop light.

'Let's get outta here,' says the driver, 'looks like there's someone needs a cop.'

When we get back to the hotel we find we are to be thrown out because the Keyboard Player has been positively identified as the one who yesterday drained the fish tank in the restaurant, killing all the trout. If that wasn't bad enough, he'd also borrowed Starsky's handcuffs. Last night a lady guest was found, hysterical, in the bar. While having a quiet Brandy Alexander as a nightcap she'd been manacled to the bar rail by a man in dark glasses who had a dying fish waving and flapping in his top pocket.

•

*85*

In the foyer of the cinema where we are playing tonight the stall that sells souvenir T-shirts is being erected. A new notice is displayed on the counter of the T-shirt stall. It reads:

DRUMMER REQUIRES LAUNDRY AND IRONING DONE, APPLY HERE.

'Say, how are you fellas enjoying your stay in the Fantasy Kingdom?' asks the waiter as he sets down the drinks on the table beside us.

The Drummer, the Colonel and myself have driven from our nearby hotel so that we can sit on the man-made beach of the Polynesian hotel in Disneyworld and drink tequila sunsets, while gentle music is piped to us through concealed speakers in fibreglass totem poles.

'It's a bit Mickey Mouse, innit,' replies the Colonel.

'Why thank you sir.'

Earlier in the afternoon we'd been on rides, like Pirates of the Caribbean, where we sat in a boat, attached to a conveyor belt, and were dragged through a trough of water a foot deep, and into a labyrinth of tunnels and caverns where mock sea battles took place in a computer-controlled sequence of booms and splashes and orange flashes that repeated itself every thirty seconds. Animated dummies of pirates jerked tankards towards their heads and tipped non-existent grog down their noses or into their ears. Or they chased wenches into houses where, hopefully, they made a better connection.

Now we sit and watch the sun sink lower and lower. No doubt the sun is watching us do the same. We go indoors, feeling groggy. In the bar the Colonel gooses a waitress and she drops her tray. A security man heads towards us. We run. The lobby of the Polynesian hotel is so massive that it contains a monorail station and tropical landscaping so vast that it makes the palm house in Kew Gardens look like a window box. We escape through the jungle and out into the car park and take off, but we're still being chased.

The Colonel is laughing his bollocks off: 'I was drunk last night, I'm drunk tonight and I'll be drunk tomorrow night. I am what I am.'

'If they catch us they'll do us,' says the Drummer.

I accelerate as fast as the great tin whale I'm driving will allow. When we get around the next bend I swing the car across a wide strip of grass and drive slowly back towards the hotel.

'Duck down,' I shout, and even in the middle of all this I am forced to laugh.

'Donald Duck!' says the Colonel.

'Get your head down,' says the Drummer, pulling him down out of sight.

Five seconds later a car rips past on the opposite side of the road, its blue flashing light illuminating the two large plastic ears attached to its roof.


In the main street of Montgomery, the Klan are out collecting money, fund raising and looking like bedsheet ghosts, except that these are frightening.

In the same Alabama town, in a shopping mall, a man dressed in a white robe (without the hood) drags a large, but hollow, wooden cross behind him, while others with him hand out tracts and collect cash. I notice that at the foot of the cross, where it drags along the ground, it runs quite smoothly. Someone has fitted a small wheel.

# 5

*I mean, what's it like to be a rock star 'n all?* . . .

I didn't know the answer to that one: the rock star is an American phenomenon. But at home, we had actually been pop stars once. It started during a January and lasted until half-way through March. We had a hit record and Oxfam did great business as people sought out clothes like ours. One day I actually saw someone dressed exactly the same as me. Stupid bastard. We'd run out and buy bottles of Cristal on the slightest pretext. The rewards of this stardom were certainly not to be sniffed at but they were sniffed at, until our little noses ran. We carried on like countless other nouveau-riche brats who delighted in winding up head waiters.

'Wot's chateaubriand, John?' we'd ask, while dumping 100-year-old armagnac into coffee.

We wouldn't even look at a bottle of wine that hadn't come covered in cobwebs from the cellar.

It was during this period that we were asked to fly to the other side of the world to play at a gigantic festival in New Zealand and, because there were only five days off in our diary for the rest of the year, this was going to be our holiday and the 'trip of a lifetime'. We were going to do it in style. The gig paid seventy grand. If there was any dosh left over at the end we'd divide it up. If there'd been any dosh left over at the end it would've been a bloody miracle.

The Drummer's home movie shows us quaffing champagne

in the Concorde departure lounge on the first leg of our trip to Singapore. The rest of the film is indecipherable as it lurches, grainy and underexposed, around the world.

There were only the four of us on this trip, along with our agent, Nigel, who'd been appointed as our tour manager, nurse and guardian. Ted Bidits was extrebely biffed dot to be goig od the drip. Nigel was a quiet and self-effacing chap, as I suppose all QPR supporters are bound to be. Now and again we both played football for the same team. He was the goalie. His game was modelled on the Ancient Mariner, 'who stoppeth one in three'.

The cabin of Concorde is long and narrow and, because of the height it flies at and the pressurization of the cabin, the windows are small like portholes. At first it gave me the impression of sitting aboard a rocket. The seats are in pairs on either side of the aisle and even these are more like the seats of a fast car than an aeroplane's. I sat with a window on one side and the Singer on the other. Our take-off was going to be delayed, so I found a book in my bag.

*Birdman* is the biography of a French maniac who built wings from plywood and canvas which he strapped across his shoulders – a sort of prototype hang-glider. In white boiler suit and crash helmet he hurled himself from planes and hurtled earthwards at 176 feet a second, ripping open his parachute at the last possible moment. The book had come from a second-hand shop in Shepherds Bush. I'd been trying to find a copy ever since my father had refused to buy me one the first time I'd seen it while on holiday in Scarborough. He had done this in the certain knowledge that, as soon as I got home, I would have tied the door of the garden shed across my back with the clothes-line and flung myself headlong from the side of the nearest tip.

The Singer looked sideways at me. He was a white-knuckle flyer and, looking over my shoulder, wasn't appreciating the photos of the Frenchman falling from the sky. The Singer believed that, while a tall and square-jawed captain had cast his cool gaze over the passengers as we'd boarded shortly before take-off and while a lazy voice reassured us that everything was all right, an unshaven loony with an eye-patch and an aluminium leg was being forced, struggling, behind the controls on the flight deck.

One pleasure I've never lost is that of seeing the world from above. Even after hundreds of flights I still prefer the window seat so that I can watch the flaps disappear to reveal a mosaic of yellows and greens below, and the black of woods, and the sun reflecting on water; or, at night, the red and white pin-points of lights from cars moving like corpuscles along the arterial roads. The enjoyment comes from the sense of detachment and of being a silent observer.

Once we were out over the sea, the captain announced that we were going supersonic. A digital speedo at the front of the passenger cabin showed our air speed in Mach numbers – Mach 1·0 being the speed of sound, around 760 miles an hour. The number rose quickly as we accelerated so that I could actually feel the seat pressing against my back just like on take-off.

And soon we were flying at twice the speed of sound. The sky was a deep indigo flecked with silver. I could even see the curvature of the earth and a light strip of blue where ordinary planes bumbled along at 37,000 feet. We were up among the stars in a very rarefied atmosphere. Not for us the standard fare, but Iranian caviare, bone china, cut glass and silverware. The Singer and I drew upon all our expert knowledge, having had caviare twice before, and declared this to be the best. I'd learned the names of one or two good wines and ordered them with unceasing regularity. If the plane went down I'd be found crawling across the desert, croaking 'Montrachet' and 'Chambertin'. The caviare was served with vodka that was held chilled in a hollowed-out block of ice. The Drummer's head appeared, in a froth of champagne bubbles, over the back of my seat.

'Cor, is that solid ice?' he said, so impressed by the presentation that he noticed the ice before the drink.

'No,' I replied. 'It's ice. To say solid ice is as stupid as saying liquid water. It's tautological.'

I'd been trying to use the word ever since I first discovered it three weeks earlier. It was one of those words I wanted to let hang in the air a little longer, so that I could admire and savour it, but the word pretentious kept getting in the way and anyway the pa had clicked on and a voice was announcing: 'Good afternoon ladies and gentlemen. Further to our safety demonstration we wish to advise you that we've just had a look and there are not enough life-jackets to go round. However our cabin staff are busy knitting –'

There was the sound of scuffling and a certain Keyboard Player was returned to his seat and given the clear understanding that any repetition of an incident like that would result in his arrest when we landed. He settled back in his seat, his face the picture of gratification.

There was an hour in transit in Bahrain where we were in danger of sobering up. Imagine it: the very first stop on our outing, an airport with no bevvy. I drank a cup of coffee and inspected a model of an oil refinery in a glass case. Then I walked slowly up to the far end of the lounge and back. I had a

Fanta and examined a model of the new airport terminal and wandered by the scenic route (it took me past a stand selling postcards) to the end of the lounge and back. Then I drank . . . No. We could reboard. I handed in my cardboard pass and got back on the plane.

This was the kind of trip, unlike all the others, that would never be repeated and I'd set out determined not to let it all pass in an alcoholic haze. Day trips would be organized. We'd see things. There'd be culture. I spent the rest of the flight and the taxi ride to Ratfles in an alcoholic haze.

Opening my eyes next morning the first thing I saw was a, ah, aaargh! I snatched the covers back over my head and rolled out the other side of the bed. Aaargh!

These were the days when we still roomed in pairs. I shared with the Singer. Last night after I'd gone to sleep he'd been out. He'd bought one of those souvenirs that are thrust under your nose at every twenty paces: a stuffed mongoose locked in combat with a giant cobra. This had been left beside my bed, with the snake coiled right over my pillow ready to strike. The Singer allowed a smile to caress his features.

(This was another point scored in a long-running game that involved playing tricks on each other – sometimes intentionally, and sometimes accidentally. I'd once scored points accidentally by leaving a jar of orange juice on the bedside table. In the morning he'd gulped down a few mouthfuls before he realized that it was a fifty-fifty mix with vodka. In another motel, I'd sat up half the night with a biro altering the pattern on the wallpaper, changing each fleur de lys until there was a sea of little gargoyles and staring faces, so that he woke up to this awful hallucination.)

We left the duty-free emporium in Singapore loaded down

with ghetto blasters, cameras and watches. The Singer had surrendered to high-powered sales talk and ended up buying a camera with a flash gun, motor wind and a telephoto lens, all in a metal case. Our whistle-stop cultural tour of Singapore took us first to the Tiger Balm Gardens, a park full of fantastic sculptures. In a pool, plaster seals, painted to look like tigers, copulated with turtles and mice and giant ants. At a quick glance it looked like a pop festival. There was a representation of the Buddhist idea of hell where people boiled in oil or had various limbs removed by a man with a saw. Funny that: being legless was the Drummer's idea of heaven. Part of the park was laid out as formal gardens where the Singer, for once overcoming his antipathy to nature, experimented with his camera and took photos of the flowers.

There was also an area that had been left wild. Inside it was hot, green and dense – like stepping into a Rousseau painting. Palm fronds pointed like daggers and big leaves the size of elephants' ears steamed and sweated. Sunlight broke through the canopy of leaves and slanted down, almost vertically, in luminous columns so that each tall tree had a spirit at its side. And there, spotlighted just above my head, was the biggest spider I hope ever to see.

We took a quick bus tour and then went on to see some traditional entertainment: the Lion Dance and some plate spinning. The Drummer volunteered to get up on stage as part of a musical act involving snakes. According to him this was no different to what he ordinarily did for a living. Beside me there was a synchronized explosion of light as the Singer managed to get the motor wind and the flash to go off together on his camera. The flash fired twice every second, taking snaps of various knees, backs of heads and his own quizzical expression, while the flickering light gave the scene the feeling of an old, silent comedy. He was utterly cack-handed when it came to machinery: a trail of broken guitar strings across the theatres of America and Europe had led us to name him *Manitas de Concreta*. His particular situation was made doubly dangerous when there were animals involved. Dogs always growled at him. And if there were one solitary mosquito in the whole of Singapore, then it would be sure to find him. I hoped there were no tigers loose. Somerset Maugham told of a tiger wandering into the bar of Raffles while he was staying there. He didn't say what the tiger was drinking.

That evening we dined in colonial splendour on the hotel veranda. After the last cognac had been drained and the bill signed we went to find a local bar. We wandered through streets where people cooked duck or sold stuffed mongooses at the throats of cobras. We bought pirated cassette tapes for a dollar each.

At midnight the streets began to liven up. We sat outside and ordered beers. Tiger beer! A woman, tall and elegant in a sparkling sheath of a dress, sailed close and sat on the Drummer's knee; she asked him in sign language if he wanted a date. She opened the front of her dress to show her tits.

'Meet her by the pawnbroker's,' said Nigel, 'and you can give her a squeeze under the balls!'

'Whaddya mean?' said the Drummer sitting there as happy as a dog with two dicks. 'Aaaargh!'

He hurled her from his knees the instant he realized that there were indeed two male organs involved, and that 'she' was one of those transvestite prostitutes famed throughout these exotic parts. We were subsequently invited to see some more traditional entertainment. Apparently there was a club where a stripper managed to get a tune out of a trumpet by playing it with her own more exotic parts.

'No thanks,' I said. 'I know a whole horn section that play like cunts.'

The next morning I woke just in time to check out. Outside the hotel the Keyboard Player was sitting behind his shades quietly nursing a mild turkey, while his suitcases were being loaded into the back of our car.

'I'll keep that with me,' he said, taking his new tape player from the bellhop and placing it on the roof of the car.

'That is one sick bird there,' indicated the Drummer. 'Look at him. He's barely maintaining.'

That morning the Drummer had been out and had a suit made to measure in three hours. In bright yellow silk with a red lining, it had a label saying 'specially made for' and his name stitched beneath. Not that anyone else would have had a suit like that made. A large blue label that said Fyffes would have been more appropriate.

'Style never goes out of fashion,' he said.

I agreed. 'Yes, and it's lucky that tomorrow you'll be able to get a hat with corks dangling from it to go with it.'

'Careful with that!' he said to the porter as his luggage was being loaded. It included a stuffed mongoose locked in combat with a cobra.

The car pulled away; there was a clatter and a crash and the driver braked. Twenty yards behind us a tape player lay in the road spewing out a ribbon of tape.

At Auckland there was an argument at immigration. By law, animals, seeds, fruits and farm produce could not be imported, so a customs official was attempting to impound the mongoose; the Drummer wasn't keen to let it go.

'I know where it'll end up,' he protested, 'at home for your kids to play with. I bet you keep 'em well supplied in your job.'

We were, eventually, let into the country.

As we drove towards town we met old Veloxes and Wyverns, Minxes, Somersets and Cambridges – the sorts of solid saloons that uncles always had. They were still rust free, so I supposed that although New Zealand looked a lot like Wales the weather must be much better. But we were on the look-out for another kind of saloon. The first pub we found was next to a vast container yard where ships were loaded. Inside we ordered pints. The locals seemed friendly. A couple of dockers, one in dungarees and a string vest, smashed pool balls round a table. It was only after a few minutes that I realized that they were women. They looked as much like men as that man in Singapore had looked like a woman.

We checked into the Intercontinental and I went straight up to the restaurant on the top floor. A brochure in my room had promised a spectacular view of the harbour.

'Sorry. You can't come in without a tie.'

'Oh, I see. So I happen to be wearing a three-hundred-quid suit and I don't get in, an' you let these ponces go swanning straight in as long as they've got a piece of coloured nylon knotted round their necks. I tell you what, pal, I've often wondered what happened to all the crap in my Auntie's mail-order catalogue that no one would ever buy. Now I know, 'cos there's ship loads of it out here.'

I ate in a Chinese restaurant, then came back and watched an episode of 'Coronation Street' nearly all the way through before I realized that I'd seen it two years earlier at home.

Lying out on the deck of a motor boat in the blazing sun,

pissed and jet lagged, is not the only way to feel wretched but it's one of the best. We had a day off to relax before the gig on the following day, and the promoter had hired a boat for us and put us out to sea. I stared, incredulous, at the name of this boat painted across its bows, *The Valium*. The promoter had also thrown in a couple of hookers who we kept busy serving drinks. Shona had a swimsuit cut away almost to her armpits, revealing that it must've been trainee day down at the Auckland bikini waxers. The heat and the drink and all that fresh air had begun to make me feel groggy when the Drummer called a meeting of the Deep End Club. This was one of the many clubs that we'd invented which had the flimsiest of membership requirements and which called occasional and informal meetings. There were only three members of this club: the Drummer, the Keyboard Player and myself. The Singer was ineligible because he was prone to get vertigo if he stood on a thick sheet of paper. When a meeting of the Deep End Club was called by one of its members, it required all of us to jump into the nearest body of water, whether it be the sea or a swimming-pool, at that instant, fully clothed or not. It was of course permitted to remove certain essential items from one's pockets. At the Drummer's call, all that was required was for us to jump into Auckland harbour on a nice sunny day. No worries.

Splash! The water was colder than I expected. It was a shock. The cold water on my body was real; the other antics would become no more than vaguely remembered larks.

(The Deep End Club had been inaugurated in Boulder, Colorado. Late one night we'd leapt into a hotel swimming-pool, fully clothed and pissed as parrots. It was a moment later when we realized that it was not the hotel we were staying in:

we'd come down the road to this one because the bar stayed open later. Outside it was several degrees below and starting to snow. We wrapped ourselves in large bath towels and wandered off in search of a cab, now members of a new club called the Three Centurions.

On another occasion we all bought white Beatle boots in a thrift store to form the White Boot Gang. On yet another tour the Twenty-Four Hour Club was conceived, membership of which meant merely staying up all night. The conversation hardly sparkled and often ended up with us watching Euro TV showing Germans in costume yodelling 'Halloo Halloo' with falcons perched on their wrists. Or we'd improvise episodes of 'Hector's House' or 'Camberwick Green', although nobody much liked being Windy Miller. We all wanted to be Captain Snort of Pippin Fort. Captain Snort played a big part in the Twenty-Four Hour Club.)

Although a helicopter had been laid on to take us to the gig, the Singer wasn't keen on it at all, so we drove out into the country to the festival site. But the Helicopter Gang went up for a short hop over the gig to see the crowds, the stage and the cars parked in the hills where sheep grazed. We promptly named the festival Chickenstock. The sides of the plexiglass bubble that was the helicopter cockpit were completely open, so that when the pilot banked hard to the left there was nothing at all between me and the ground a thousand feet below except the nylon strap holding me in; I felt just like Bird-man.

Once back down, I swapped my stage pass for a go on one of the little golf carts that the stewards scurried around the site on. I drove around the fields for an hour, ignoring the requests over the walkie-talkie to bring it back. Even at this moment I somehow couldn't stop travelling. And then, in the middle of a field, I came across a chemical toilet. On the door was stencilled: PORT-A-LOO, FOR THE EXCLUSIVE USE OF – Underneath was our name and a single yellow star. I wondered if this was how Hunter S. Thompson would've felt if ever he'd discovered his hamburger stand called the American Dream.

Travelling light, we hadn't brought any crew or equipment with us, so I had to tune my own guitars. I spent a therapeutic half hour sitting, putting the guitar in and out of tune so that I could keep watching the stroboscopic display on the tuner gradually resolve itself and become still. Eventually we changed into stage clothes and caught the cart to the stage. The opening song was a new one and involved only the Singer and the Keyboard Player. It was full of dramatic stops and starts. The Drummer and I waited in the wings for our cue.

'Is that it? 'As 'e finished?'

We ran on stage just as they lurched into a last verse and tried to melt backwards into the wings unseen.

Then we really were on. As I hit the first note, one hundred thousand people in the audience simultaneously broke wind, or that's what it sounded like. Could this truly be the best equipment they had? I tried to get some kind of workable sound out of it while attempting to convince the Aussie monitor mixer that for me to be able to hear the drums and vocals would be no bad thing.

(Like all groups, we generally played so loud on stage that any acoustic sound, like drums or voices, had to be played back to the stage through a system of speakers that could be mixed individually for us, so that each of us could hear what was happening on the other parts of the stage.)

And then our ninety minutes were up. A couple of quick

encores and a firework display preceded a wagon train of VW campers that began slowly to move out.

The next scheduled stop on our 'holiday' was Peru. Yes it was, I'm afraid to say. Or, it was going to be, until the Singer got wind that the flight from Auckland to Lima was going to be on a DC 10. The tickets had to be changed which meant having to fly via Los Angeles on a 747, a minor detour of a few thousand miles. Thinking about it, it wasn't much sillier than the three successive gigs we'd once done, which took us from Exeter on a Friday, to Edinburgh the following night, and back down to Plymouth for the Sunday. Still, it was appropriate that it was our agent who had to re-route the plane tickets.

We drove from LAX, up La Cienaga, to the Château Marmont, an ice-cream castle of a hotel that has seen better days. It sits in no man's land, right on the boundary where the flat sprawl of forty suburbs looking for a city meets the canyons, where the wealthy and successful perch their A-frames on stilts and try not to think about earthquakes. From my hotel window I could see the billboards stretching away down Sunset: a file of gigantic, grinning personas.

I wandered back down the hill and had a beer at Barney's Beanery where they stocked a hundred and more different kinds of beer from all over the world. On their list Yorkshire was counted as a country in its own right. Barney's was such an archetypal American diner that one Dutch pop-artist had even built a small replica of it. In his version all the customers had clocks for heads. At the next table two Californian versions of Jack-the-lad discussed the finer points of playing pool until finally they decided to play. The long, slim cases were opened, cues were chalked and the balls were racked up. The first shot sent the cue ball skidding off the edge of the pack and straight into a pocket. In off. But it didn't stop their clocks.

When I got back to the hotel the Singer was in the room talking to a guy called Doug. He too was a singer. He was with a lightweight American pop outfit, the Knack, who were staying at the same hotel. There was an argument in progress about music: Tamla, soul and reggae. Doug made the fatal mistake of saying that he'd listened to reggae long before it had become fashionable in England.

'My mom used ιο play Harry Belafonte records all the time.'

'Harry Belafonte! Reggae!' we chorused.

The piss taking moved from the playful to the merciless and he was forced to leave.

In the morning we were so far gone that the door had to be battered down before we could be roused. While waiting outside for our transport back to LAX a Porsche pulled up to park and accidentally knocked over the Singer's suitcase. His Dr Marten put a dent in the door of the Porsche. Another argument broke out.

We drove out to the airport past funny oil pumps that looked like big metal birds pecking at the ground.

The Drummer was unusually quiet.

'Got a bit of a turkey 'av we?' I said.

'I thought I'd got away with it at first,' he said, 'but it'd only gone away to look for twigs. I think it's going to build a nest on my head so it can move in permanently.'

Varig Airlines' flight to Lima did us proud. There was pheasant or filet mignon for lunch and even bottles of Gevrey-Chambertin. I looked over to the seat behind me.

'How are the accounts looking Nige?'

He didn't look up.

'Nige! I said how's the bunce holding out. What're the accounts looking like?'

'A bit hazy, old boy. A bit hazy.'

'Gentlemen please,' said the chief steward, 'I must ask you, no more wine, please.'

'Whaddya mean?' said Nigel, 'we're not drunk!'

'No gentlemen. But please, or we shall not make a profit on the flight.'

The Lima Sheraton is built on the site of an old prison. Built from bare, grey slabs, it is even laid out like a prison with the floors in a series of tiers opening on to a central area. Having arrived and checked in during the afternoon, we went out, taking a cab to the local market. At first glance it looked just like Kensington Market with Peruvian woollies everywhere. I soon got used to a stray hand dipping into my pockets every five minutes: usually the street kid's accomplice would try to distract me by pestering me to buy one of the cheap souvenirs. You needed to be careful where you walked, too. The mongrels that lay asleep, or dying, would bite and offer you a catalogue of diseases.

The traffic looked like a scrapyard come to life. In Peru there is no MOT (neither is it permitted to import cars) and there is a constant racket, with dark, belching fumes from exhausted cars. These heaps of rust, doors missing, wings hanging off, clug and phop along rusty roads into rusty hills.

A brand-new Mercedes gleamed white past us: another bribe had beaten the system. A constant racket.

Just out of town is the Temple of the Moon Goddess. Beyond, standing atop a hill, was such an astonishing view that I wanted to memorize it completely. Slowly I turned a full circle, trying to take in every detail in front of me without becoming lost in the way I was describing it to myself: the water; the oil refinery; the town; and then a distinct dividing line where suddenly the land is flat and featureless; beyond, the temple; silver tanks there, a white stone here, a rusting Coke sign; the breeze; the fading light; and the sound of the distance.

I was, I thought, a long way from home.

In the evening we found the only French restaurant in town for dinner. It wasn't very good and it certainly wasn't cheap. The customers were the military, the police and gangsters doing business together while wining and dining their mistresses or hookers. Outside the restaurant we met a Scotsman who invited us to his party, if we'd bring a bottle of Scotch. It turned out that a bottle of Scotch here cost ten times what it did in Scotland.

'What are you doing in Peru?' I asked, striking up a conversation in the car.

'What are *you* doing in Peru?'

I suppose it was a stupid question.

At his apartment, a few people were introduced while the whisky was poured out. Then like a kid who'd caught sight of the presents on Christmas morning I saw, over in one corner, piled up on a table, a small hill of sparkling white powder. Here was enough bat food for a Transylvanian cricket team. And everyone who lived here wanted Scotch. Typical.

'Och, we do a run a few times a year. Go through Spain. Ye cannie give the stuff away here.'

'You can!'

'Go ahead, help yersel'.'

It was hard to believe. I shovelled far too much on to a corner of a credit card.

'That'll do nicely.'

No it wouldn't. Hell's teeth! This was the real'thing.

For the next half an hour it was a question only of whether my heart or my brain would pack up first. I stood outside gripping the railing on the balcony and watching a clock on a nearby building. Both hands seemed frozen. I might be standing up dead. If I saw the clock get round to three I'd be all right. Outside, the gardens and the street kept taking on the appearance of a Christmas card. Everything seemed iced over. But it was lush and green. I kept muttering stupid puns about Christmas to myself. I was crackers! I was out of my tree! Rigid as the metal railing, I felt as if it were growing up through my hands and arms so that I had a cast-iron skeleton and a steel skull. My eyes stared like a fool's and my jaw stayed tense and tight.

'Better try and get some sleep,' said the Singer as we lay back on our hotel beds.

'Yeah.'

The texture of the ceiling wasn't that interesting after a couple of hours. There were only so many imaginings that could be projected on to it. Slowly a simple question that had been forming beneath the turmoil of imagination could be ignored no longer.

'How on earth did I end up here?' it went. Again and again.

'Out of the question,' said Nigel to the kid hustling us to buy his souvenirs as we waited at the airport for our flight to Rio. Yet we all had a pocketful of grubby notes that were no use, except to a hungry Peruvian kid. The Drummer had repossessed his mongoose on leaving Auckland and carried it with him protectively, everywhere. He'd bought himself a poncho. And he wore a straw hat. He thought he looked like

Clint Eastwood. He looked like a prat. There was a crash. The
Keyboard Player stood in a circle of broken glass. A pool of
clear liquid formed around his shoes and in the middle of this
pool, looking up forlornly, was a little worm. He'd dropped a
bottle of Mezcal.

In Rio, the Singer took to his bed and stayed there for the
duration, insisting that it was all because of a dodgy bit of fish.
It was either Peruvian hayfever, or, being a hypochondriac,
he'd been driven sick with the worry that finally he'd run out
of illnesses.

I walked out of the hotel into the crowd strolling along the
front where a crescent of white hotels stretched away for
miles, as far as Sugar Loaf Mountain. The carnival was starting
the following week. We'd miss that, but already there were
bands out warming up.

'Hey mister, your shoes. I clean your shoes.'

'No thanks,' I said to the boy.

'But mister, look, sheet.'

I looked at my shoes. Unbelievably, sitting squarely on each
toecap was something that looked like a Walnut Whip. The
spiral whirls of crap couldn't have been more skilfully done by
a pastry chef.

'OK, get it off.'

The boy kneeled down and wiped my shoes with a rag. He
wouldn't take less than a dollar.

More lorryloads of thrashing percussionists thundered past.
Rhythms like these are usually described as infectious. Like all
infections, after a few hours you begin to wish they'd go
away. At the edge of the beach huge waves reared up suddenly
and crashed down almost on the same spot, while the beach
itself was a sea of goalposts. Every pitch was being used. A

hundred, a thousand, games were being played by skinny, brown youths hoping to escape, in groups of eleven, from a life of poverty. The sand was too deep for the ball to roll, so the ball had to be chipped or headed accurately from player to player. It was a football scout's paradise.

'Excuse senhor, I clean your shoes.'

Two more whirls had appeared on my shoes. Another shoeshine boy was ready to wipe them off for another dollar. This time I saw his mate, a little way off, stirring a paint tin with a stick to keep the mixture of imitation dog-do at its optimum consistency ready to dollop on to the next pair of unsuspecting feet.

'No,' I said, 'I'll keep it. I like it. Thank you very much.'

I continued walking. The boys chased after me. My shoes drew a few stares from passing Brazilians but it was worth the slight embarrassment to see the reaction.

'But look. Look!'

I stopped, bent down, and carefully took one whirl off a shoe. The boys' faces were wide in disbelief. Nobody had ever done this before.

'Mmmm,' I said, 'sure looks like shit. Sure feels like shit. Smells a bit like shit too. Good job I didn't step in it.'

'But look! But look! You are not American?'

I walked up and away from the beach and into the hills. The luxury hotels gave way to scruffier streets. A group of children sat at the edge of a fountain sniffing glue in a paper bag and swaying in a street lamp's glow. Another child climbed out of the brown water and stretched his shiny wet body along the ground. Further along there were foodstores and chemists, greasy lunch bars and cheap hotels. Then I found a shanty town that didn't appear on my tourist map. Rags of children ran barefoot chasing a cat that scurried and cowered under the shell of a burnt-out Volkswagen.

The statue of Christ on the mountain top appeared to look down impartially on both rich and poor alike and then the clouds closed around it once again. Nobody smiled. I felt uncomfortable in my laundered shirt, with a new watch and camera. I was in the wrong place. As I walked back down the hill I turned a corner to face maybe a hundred young men returning from playing football on the beach and with them a few younger boys carrying tins and sticks. All wore cut-off jeans. None wore shoes or shirts. None were overweight. They jostled me, jeered a bit. But for some reason they didn't rob me. I wouldn't have blamed them if they had.

A day later we were on Concorde again, this time via Dakar to Paris where we were squirted through the tunnels and tubes of the Charles de Gaulle. The last lap of luxury was an airbus back to London. There were three hundred businessmen in dark suits and reeking of aftershave, and there were five of us (one of whom looked like a giant banana in a cape, carrying a stuffed mongoose).

As a final flourish of flash Nigel had arranged for a white Roller to collect us at Heathrow. We stepped in and collapsed back. The driver started telling the joke about the man who finds a plastic golf tee in the back of a Roller and doesn't know what it is.

'It's what you put your balls on before you drive off,' we chanted wearily.

# 6

*Hey man, is this the first band you've been in? . . .*

When I first left the north of England and came down to London with the other Roadrunners (Moody the guitarist, Prickly Wilf the singer and Dave the drummer) I was hungry for success. Soon, I was just plain hungry.

I woke up when I heard Moody and Prickly Wilf leaving for their part-time jobs at the handbag factory on Holloway Road. The curtains were still drawn and a single blue bulb had been left on. It glared, sickly and pale, and flattened every feature of the room making it look like the picture on a TV screen.

Dave was preparing to hitch all the way to Scotland to see the only girl who'd ever 'let him'. He was going to be a drummer only until he made enough money to start his own road-haulage business. He got out of bed still wearing his trousers and a silver lurex shirt that had been on him so long that the armpits had gone rusty, and grunted a hello or goodbye – I couldn't tell which. He had a red freckled face, ginger hair and beard. All he needed was a helmet with two horns. He put on the donkey jacket that said TARMAC on the back. He loved that donkey jacket almost as much as he loved his drumkit.

'Ow you!'

I looked up.

'Keep off them fuckin' drums while arm away, or al fuckin' ploat yer.'

The girl in Invercockieleekie had a lot to look forward to.

It was not easy to keep off them fuckin' drums. In a top-floor bedsit that already held four beds, a chest of drawers, a wardrobe, cooker and washbasin, there was set up – bang in the middle – a drumkit. It was a red glitter Trixon kit with two bass drums, five toms, and several ride, crash and zizzle cymbals. My ribs still ached and showed a bruise from where Dave had thumped me for sneezing near his kit.

'What's the difference between you and a pair of Dr Scholl's sandals?' I muttered under my breath as he left. 'Well, Dave, Dr Scholl's sandals buck up the feet, whereas you . . .'

I got up. I was hungry. On the mantelpiece was only the rancid remains of a packet of margarine and the best part of a bag of flour. They stood next to the battery razor my mother had given me last Christmas, which I'd soon be old enough to use. Until another gig came in I'd be living on flour and water pancakes fried in margarine. I wasn't going to work in a bloody handbag factory and end up like Moody, who hid his wages in an Oxo tin whose secret location was, like a pirate radio station, constantly changing. I was a professional musician. Later I would stroll down to Mac Fisheries and nick a couple of yoghurts and a malt loaf.

There was a knock and, before I could answer, the door opened. It was Edmund McGonagle, the landlord's gopher.

'Well?'

'I haven't got any, Edmund.' There was no point in my making further excuses or promising to pay next week.

'Well then, yers'll all have to be out o' here by the weekend and that's that,' he said. 'Unless . . .'

'Unless what?'

'Unless we come to . . . an arrangement.'

'What sort of arrangement? Two verses, chorus, middle eight, chorus, verse, chorus, chorus, out.'

'What the pock'r yers talkin' about,' said McGonagle getting angry. 'Are you taking the pockin' piss?'

'No, I'm not,' I replied quickly. 'What d'you want?'

'I need the van for a while. I'll knock a month off the arrears. Fair enough?'

'Why, what's up with your van?'

'It's pocked.'

McGonagle haɑ a job on the side. Apart from working for the landlord, he ferried gangs of navvies about North London from site to site. He'd borrowed the Roadrunners' van once before and never even bothered to take our gear out, or put anything over it. Half a dozen pissed-up Paddies left behind an Irish sea of mud, sand and cement. It had taken Dave two days to clean his drum cases, but he never once threatened violence to Edmund. McGonagle was an old Teddy boy and though he had only the receding remains of a quiff, he still wore shoes with vicious points that were curled and split from kicking people.

'Me van's pockin' pocked,' he went on, 'and I've got a special contract.'

'What d'you mean?' I asked.

'I've got to go out of London, pick a few things up, drop a few things off.'

Here a picture formed instantly. It was a picture of me sitting next to McGonagle in a bright and cosy transport café, tucking into mixed grill with all the trimmings (a 'motorway pile-up') and a large mug of tea.

'I'll give you a hand to get the stuff out of the van,' I said.

Our gear didn't look at all secure, disguised to look like

something or other under the tarpaulin that McGonagle had slung over it. Still, as long as we were back by the time the day shift at the handbag factory clocked off.

'Where're we going?' I said, as we drove out through Kingston.

'Southampton.'

'What! Southampton's a hundred miles,' I choked. 'What've we got to go there for?'

'Wellies.'

It was late morning when we arrived on the outskirts of Southampton and drove on to a vast building site where a nuclear power station was being built. The wind whipped in across the Solent as we threaded between deep, water-filled craters across the churned-up clay to an enormous shed. The site foreman opened the doors.

There are prizes to be won by people who can guess how many marbles there are in a large jar, or how many baked beans there are in a bath. How many wellingtons were there in this shed? Your guess is as good as mine. As we were loading them, three times I got past two hundred and then lost count.

During the loading I found out that a system operated where each workman on the site had three pairs of wellies allotted to him. One pair was the pair he was wearing. The second was the pair that had worn out and was now in need of repair. There was also a third pair that had already been reconditioned and was ready to replace the current pair when they'd worn down. We were to take away the worn wellies to have their soles remoulded.

The Roadrunners' van was an old Thames 7 cwt (and, if the light caught it a certain way, you could still read where we'd sprayed over MOTHER'S PRIDE). There wasn't a lot of room inside it: by the time the last pair of wellies had been wedged in they filled the van right up to the roof, and their weight pressed the suspension down flat against the back axle.

Heading north along the A30 Edmund's transistor crackled away on the dashboard: Canned Heat, The Beatles, The Who – 'On the Road Again', 'Tomorrow Never Knows', 'I Can See for Miles'. It was one of the times when music genuinely did provide the soundtrack for life. As we drove straight past one transport café after another, McGonagle could hold out no longer. He took some sandwiches wrapped in greaseproof from his pocket, ate one, and grudgingly offered me one.

'Only one, now.'

All the way to Southampton and back for a poxy cheese sandwich.

But the day had brightened up. The sun was out. It was hot. The subtle fragrance of Old Wellington filled the van, even with the windows down.

'Where're we going with this lot then?' I inquired.

'Hatfield.'

Hatfield is thirty miles north of London.

'That's cutting it a bit fine, isn't it?'

We would only just have had time to drop this lot off, then get back to Finsbury Park and put the gear back in the van before the others got back from work.

'We've got to drop this lot off in Hatfield?' I said, hoping that I'd misunderstood. I had.

'Arr, now.'

'What does that mean?'

'We've just got to pick up one or two more, that's all.'

'But there's no room.'

'It's all right now. There won't be so many. We'll squeeze 'em in. It'll be all right.'

'What, and then bring them back to London and drop ...' My voice dropped away, along with any likelihood that it was going to be simple.

'Arr, now.'

'Where?'

'Preston.'

The next load was forced in between the first one. Then the wellingtons were stacked up: in the driver's cab, round the wheel arches, in any gap under the seats, around the sides of the seats, under the dashboard, along the dashboard. A pair of small wellies was put inside the glove box. A few more were piled around the gearlever and the handbrake, leaving just enough room for the levers to be operated. More wellies were made into a cushion for me, then a backrest, and then armrests. And finally, when the last pair was on board, McGonagle banged a few extra pounds of air in the tyres and we lurched off towards Preston docks because, as I'd since found out, all the best welly refurbishers are in Belfast. It was slow progress towards Preston. We were dangerously overloaded and McGonagle thought it better to avoid the motorway.

'What about a cup of tea, or something to eat?' I said hopefully.

'I've only got enough pockin' money to get the petrol. I don't get pockin' well paid until I've done the pockin' job.'

Suddenly I found myself upside down, on my back, as the wall of wellingtons tumbled around and over and under me, taking me down into a fetishist's paradise: a moving sea of smelly black rubber. By the time McGonagle had pulled me free and out through the passenger window to dry land, it had become clear what had happened. We stood and stared long and hard at the tattered remnants of the back tyre before either of us brought up the matter of the spare wheel because, as we both well knew, the spare wheel was in the back of the van – right inside, deep inside, underneath all those pockin' wellies.

It was just beginning to get dark and we had stacked the worst part of half the wellies neatly at the side of the road next to a sign telling us that we were seven miles from Manchester Airport, when we dug out the spare wheel and rolled it out to the side of the road. We stood and stared long and hard at the wheel before either of us brought up the subject of the jack. Half an hour later we discovered that there was no jack with which to lift up the van.

'Go then,' said Edmund, 'and see if you can find a jack.'

There were no houses round about but happily McGonagle felt sure I'd find a garage just down the road, while he stayed and guarded our cargo. Few cars passed me; not one of them stopped to give me a lift. But after twenty minutes' walk down the road I did indeed find a service station that had a car jack. The mechanic wouldn't let me take it without a deposit. I had no money, no driving licence, no watch. In fact I had nothing to leave him. As McGonagle was fond of telling me, I didn't have a pot to piss in.

It was dark by now and I almost fell over the van before I saw it. McGonagle handed me the watch his fiancée, Josie, had bought him as an engagement present. I walked the two miles back to the garage, gave over the watch and returned with the jack.

The van was raised up. The wheel with the punctured tyre was removed, and the spare wheel didn't fit! That bastard Dave! How? Why? Vague explanations offered themselves.

He'd mixed up the spare wheels at a garage? He'd bought the van like that and he just didn't know? It was the spare wheel of our old Bedford Dormobile?

'So now what do we pockin' do?'

Well, what we had to do of course was to get a wheel that did fit. This was the kind of situation that calls forth all that is most noble and courageous in man.

'Where can we nick one from?'

Where was there, nearby, where there would be a lot of cars and vans parked, and where we'd be able to find the wheel we needed? We both looked up at the airport sign.

'Come on then,' said McGonagle.

'Aren't we forgetting something?'

We couldn't just have left the wellies piled up at the side of the road; after all, somebody might've walked off in them. They were reloaded and the back door of the van was locked. We were only a few yards nearer the airport when we heard a creak, a groan, a snapping sound and the shearing of metal as the borrowed jack gave way under the weight of the wellies that had been put back. Edmund was wondering what he could say to Josie about the watch.

'Pockin' shut up!' he said, before I'd even spoken.

Airports, before the era of terrorism, weren't unfriendly places. But I didn't know that then because I hadn't ever been on a plane. There was a single security man on the gate and he was there only to make sure that people paid to park. The fence around the carpark and the few floodlights did nothing to stop us getting in unseen. Apart from having to deal with that cocktail of nausea and elation that is swallowed when you find yourself doing anything that you don't want to get caught doing, finding a van and stealing the wheel and jack was easy.

Subsequently, the important thing was to stay uncaught, but McGonagle took it to extremes. As we retraced our route, every time we saw the headlights of an approaching car from whatever direction, he would hurl the wheel and jack over a hedge or into a ditch. After the car had passed it was my job to scramble around in the dark and brambles to retrieve them.

It started to rain.

A black square can simply be a black square, or it can be a picture of a chimney sweep chasing a black cat around a coal cellar at midnight. Or it can be two people unloading a few hundred pairs of wellingtons to stand in wet heaps in the middle of nowhere in the middle of the night.

And then, the wheel was on!

The van was safely on the ground and nearly all the wellingtons reloaded when a police car on night patrol stopped to see what was afoot. The policemen got out and began to make inquiries. McGonagle, with all the shiftiness of a petty criminal and all the guilt of a lapsed Catholic, began babbling a half-arsed story about breaking down and then having no spare wheel and having to ring up his brother in Manchester who had the same kind of van and who'd just driven out and helped us put it on and oh yes very definitely and certainly it was from his brother that he'd got the wheel to be sure. If it was an innocent breakdown before, it was a nervous breakdown now. By the time he'd finished his explanation anyone would have arrested him on the spot. But the Plod couldn't be bothered with him.

Now we'd been up nearly twenty-four hours. I'd walked thirty miles and eaten a cheese sandwich. We drove, carefully, to the nearest parking spot and went to sleep.

A crowd of dockworkers had gathered round us, pissing

themselves laughing, as the black rubber boots kept coming out of the van to be loaded into the container that was to take them to Belfast. That done, all we had to do was to load the contents of the container from Ireland that was waiting for us over on the other side of the docks and take them back down to Hatfield, and Southampton.

Why there should have been even more wellies than we'd just off-loaded I couldn't guess. By the time that every last one had been crowbarred into place and forty-two pounds of air had been put in each tyre it was midday and the sun was hot and high. As we went slowly through the outskirts of Preston I mapped out a route, avoiding major roads, that would take us over the Pennines in a more or less straight line back towards London. By mid-afternoon we were on a B road in Derbyshire. McGonagle's caginess had passed through confidence to cockiness and then that black pool of rubber opened up again and I dived in.

On this occasion, both the front tyres had gone. One had burst and caused the other to do likewise. In the middle of the Pennines, with no spare wheel, we had to leave a note under the windscreen wiper: THIS VAN AND THESE WELLIES BELONG TO MCGONAGLE, 4 HENRY ROAD, LONDON N4.

We started walking again. There was no lift for us and we kept walking until we reached a bus shelter. McGonagle sat down while I stood trying to get a ride from any car that passed.

I stood.

And I stood.

By the time it was dark, I had begun to get light-headed. Out of the corner of my eye, I saw Edmund crossing himself.

Then he stood for an hour.

Two cars passed.

And then another hour.

There were headlights in the distance. McGonagle walked out and stood, motionless, in the middle of the road, his arms outstretched, prepared to stop the lorry or die. The lorry stopped and we scrambled in immediately, and then made our plea. I slept all the way back.

The following afternoon, when I was making my way down to Mac Fisheries, I passed a Ford Thames van that was standing on bricks. Its two front wheels were missing. Three days later McGonagle rolled into London with his thirty quid.

A few weeks later the Roadrunners ran out of road. On the way to a forty-quid gig in Ipswich the gearbox dropped out of the van leaving a trail of cogs along a half-mile stretch of the A12. Prickly Wilf and Dave lost the toss and had to stay with the van while Moody and I hitched back to town. It was the last time we ever saw that ginger-headed bastard of a drummer. As the saying goes, 'When the going gets tough, the tough bugger off back home and carry on being apprentice welders.' McGonagle borrowed his brother-in-law's Morris Oxford and towed the van back to town. We got our gear back. He kept the van.

We began to sell off everything we could do without. The green satin stage shirts whose ruffled fronts made us look like triffids went to one of the Scottish bands that lived on the ground floor of the house. Jackets, trousers, shoes: everything went, until I had only the clothes I stood up in and my guitar. I knew one day it would all seem funny, didn't I?

Soon two men from the finance company came to repossess Prickly Wilf's p.a. columns.

'No hard feelings boys,' he said. 'Fancy a cup of coffee before you go?'

Moody and I exchanged a quick glance. There is usually one person in a group whose role or whose turn it is to be picked on. (Before we came to London the Roadrunners had been five. Joe Bradley, a lorry driver, had been our manager and his younger brother Colin was the keyboard player. We didn't want a keyboard player, at least not with Colin's haircut and a poxy Woolworth's organ. So we called him Booker T Bradley and picked on him mercilessly.) Now there were only three of us, Moody and I had started to pick on Wilf. One day we found him hiding in a wardrobe to eavesdrop on what we might say about him. After that we'd started adding scouring-powder to his tin of powdered milk. Wilf was spooning this very mixture into the coffee he'd made for the men from the finance company.

'It's got a bit of a tang to it, that Marvel, hasn't it?' said the older of the two men.

His mate sent a mouthful spraying across the room. 'He's bloody well trying to poison us!'

Wilf found another band. Moody went back home, 'to study classical guitar'.

'Are you by any chance a bass guitarist?' said the youth who came into the guitar shop where I'd just pinned my request for work.

His hair was long, bleached blond, permed and backcombed. Sitting atop it was a huge floppy hat with a scarf tied around it. He wore knee-length boots, trousers, shirts, waistcoats and more scarves. It looked as if he were wearing two of everything – kingfisher, peacock, vermilion, lemon, all wrapped in an old fur coat. From the middle of this psychedelic jumble sale two myopic eyes peered through gold granny specs. I noticed that even his fingers were dyed and speckled with the same bright colours.

'Our bass player's let us down,' he explained in a thick West Country accent, which, by association, turned his hair to straw and lent him the image of a scarecrow. 'And we've got a gig in Carnaby Street on Saturday, when they switch on the Christmas lights.'

I didn't find out that his name was Ken until we were in the taxi, half way to Battersea, where the rest of the group were waiting to start rehearsing. I'd already found out that there was a few quid in it.

'What's the group called?' I asked.

'The Yellow Passion Loaf,' he replied. From the tone of his voice it was clear who'd thought that one up.

I recognized the drummer and the organist, 'Ray' and 'Sticky', old pros who'd been on the club circuit for years.

'Why Sticky?' I asked naïvely.

''Cos I like sticking it up,' came the reply.

Tim, the lead guitarist, gave him a disparaging look. It was Tim's group. Tim had an older brother in a group that was doing well. (At last I found that I knew someone who knew someone who'd made it.) Because of his brother's success Tim had been able to get the money to start his own group from their father, who ran a chain of hairdressing salons in Jersey. Tim had an even bigger perm than Ken and wore a white silk shirt with a big bow on the front and with billowing sleeves. We shook hands.

'What's this one called?' I said preparing to jot down the chord changes of a song.

'Sunnybop Farm,' said Ken. From the tone of his voice there was no need to ask who'd written the lyrics.

While I tried to find my way through the forests of toffee trees and down rivers of lemonade that grew up and flowed round Sunnybop Farm, Ken was busy behind us, hanging up a screen made of several bedsheets he'd sewn together. In front of us he assembled a platform made up of two stepladders with a plank across the top of them. A slide projector was placed on the plank and aimed at the bedsheets. Slides were prepared: first a smear of oil on a small sheet of glass, then a few drops of different coloured inks which were then sandwiched in another piece of glass. Once inside the projector the heat from the lamp made the oily mixture swirl about and a technicolour vomit of giant amoeba and fried eggs swam over us and on the sheets behind us. Ken stood beneath the plank with a look of satisfaction as his art appeared before him. He didn't notice the ink dripping on to his head.

Before the end of the week I'd moved into one of the bedsits in the Kensington house where the group lived. There was just enough room for me to open the door to get into my room.

As I lay on my bed I could study the wrinkles in the plastic sheet that covered most of the ceiling, which was supposed to keep the leaks off me while I slept all day. The three-pounds-a-week rent would be paid out of the kitty, held by Tim. Tim rented the entire basement level, which he'd painted purple. Mr Fish leather coats hung from his clothes rail, an Aubrey Beardsley original hung over his bed, and a pair of bush-babies scampered around. No doubt he'd decided to invest some of his father's money like this so that the trappings of our eventual success wouldn't take him by surprise. This hadn't left a lot of money over for a van to go to gigs in.

That night was spent in Ken's room where I listened for the

umpteenth time to 'Interstellar Overdrive' if only to drown out the sound of Tim's guitar playing drifting up from below. He was one of those guitarists who thought that the harder you hit a guitar string and the harder you pressed down on the fretboard with the other hand the better it would sound. His playing was as fluid as a rock; finger vibrato was non-existent. Notes were bent too sharp and then died flat, the agony being prolonged by an echo unit. He thought that the Blues was something that had been invented that week by Jimi Hendrix.

In the morning Ken's mum stopped by to fry him a large plate of chips for his breakfast while I went off to find the communal bathroom that served the ground floor. I gasped in shock. The bath was filled with blood and limbs that were bloated, twisted and mangled. A closer look revealed that it wasn't a hideous murder but several pairs of trousers left by someone to dye scarlet in the bath. My first suspect was the man with the coloured fingers.

'Those trousers anything to do with you Kenneth?'

Of course they were. He'd bought a job lot of old cricket flannels from a warehouse in the City. On an old treddle sewing machine his mum tapered the inside legs down as far as the knee, then Ken dyed them and knocked them out as loon pants for three quid a pair in Kensington Market.

'I'll use the bathroom upstairs,' I said.

The first floor bathroom was full of turquoise trousers. The next floor had orange ones. Top floor, purple.

By Saturday a half-hour set of seven songs had been learnt. We were set up in a shop doorway in Carnaby Street. The Christmas lights had been switched on, but just as Tim was about to hit the opening chords a man who looked a bit like my Dad leapt at him and grabbed the pendants hanging round his neck.

'What's this?' he demanded angrily. 'What's this? What d'you call this?' he repeated, his anger making him inarticulate.

It was the Iron Cross he'd taken offence at. He tried to snap it from around Tim's neck but the chain didn't break. The man wrestled with the chain and Tim was pulled stumbling forward, the guitar bashing against the mike stand and starting an atonal guitar frenzy. The man stalked off. Despite all this, or maybe because of it, a watching agency booker offered us a month's residency at the new Club le Happening in Marseilles.

I was in a room that was swinging from side to side sending bottles sliding along the table top. It was an ordinary cross-Channel ferry that we travelled out on but, because it was the first time I had left familiar territory, it was almost magical. The moonlight caught the water that was thrown back by the bows and turned it into a shower of diamonds. I was prepared to ignore the white scum floating along in the ship's wake.

I choked out some schoolboy French that secured a cab from Gare du Nord to Gare de Lyon. The train journey to Marseilles took twenty-seven hours and we must've made every stop on the line. The train was packed and we had to share the compartment with two US Marines who never stopped taking the piss out of Ken. I went and stood in the corridor watching the mustard-coloured houses and the pollarded trees and the thousand things I'd never seen before.

The new Club le Happening was an old Club something else, probably the Club le Twist. It may have recently changed its name but the décor and the furniture, the clientele and the atmosphere were well worn. We were greeted by the owner, a Madame Armando, who was all gold dangling things, Gucci and orange make-up. Two hours after meeting her we were calling her Mrs Armadillo.

We were shown to two barely-furnished rooms over the club where we were to live mainly on bread and cheese supplemented by whatever we could scrounge from the kitchen. Our three nightly sets consisted of the same seven songs each time. They were padded out with instrumental meanderings and punctuated by continual requests for us to turn it down and by complaints from the patrons who were unlucky enough to sit beneath Ken's plank.

In between sets Sticky was as glued to the barstool as his companions were to their fur coats. The only conventionally good-looking one amongst us, he played the gigolo and found women who looked just like Madame Armando to buy his drinks and take him to dinner. Once I tried to butt in and ponce a drink but when Sticky's companion saw me approaching she broke out in a fit of laughter:

''Ow are you Monsieur le Ghost?' she cackled. 'Ho! Ho! Monsieur le Ghost.'

Being sensitive about teenage spots it was my habit to cover my face in talcum powder, and the ultra-violet light of the dance floor must've given me an unearthly appearance.

Sticky's woman friend was married to a plastic surgeon. She had her own key to the pill cabinet where the tranquillizers and the painkillers were kept and she fed Sticky pills with inhibition-loosening and aphrodisiac effects. After a couple of those it would take him all his efforts to stay awake and his legs could've been sawn off without his ever noticing. I wondered what the point was of having fun that can neither be felt, nor remembered. Then I asked if I could have one.

A few days later my schoolboy French was needed again: to get Sticky to the clap clinic, where we sat all afternoon waiting for him to be attended to. After I'd slowly translated all the notices and the posters, I went off to find some coffee and sandwiches. When I got back Sticky had gone. After half an hour he still hadn't emerged from the examination room.

I asked a nurse; Sticky hadn't been seen. We went looking for him together and eventually found him asleep on a gynae-cologist's couch, laid back with his feet resting in the stirrups.

Against doctor's orders, Sticky went out drinking but now he had to buy his own drinks. I joined him on a search for cheaper bars. We staggered through the low life of the Latin area. I fell over a parked motor bike and Sticky was spectacu-larly sick, leaving a previous bouillabaisse all over a jukebox. Finding our way back home we came across the headquarters of the Foreign Legion. Giggling stupidly we went up to the front door and rang the doorbell. It was then I noticed the face staring out of the sentry box a yard to my right.

The next day Madame sent us home: we were still playing too loud and ink-spattered customers were still complaining.

Feeling no loyalty to a group who played songs about toffee trees I went looking for another gig. I got the addresses of successful musicians by being able to read letters upside-down on agents' and record-company desks, and by looking in address books when people were out of the room.

I walked first to South Kensington and knocked on the door of Jeff Beck's flat. When the door was opened I demanded the job as the bass player he was looking for. I was too late but he let me in and gave me an avuncular talk.

'Just as long as you can play the guitar well, you'll never be out of a job.'

I practised for nearly a week.

I went to John Mayall's flat in Royal Oak and demanded to be installed as a Bluesbreaker. On his living room floor lay a bass drum head that he was in the process of painting. It had a pseudo-Aztec design in which his own name featured most prominently. He too offered me advice while he began picking at a plate of food that looked like it was left over from yesterday.

'A Blues band is just like a boogie-woogie piano,' he said in his reedy, nasal voice. 'The bass player is like the left hand. You've got to be there, hitting the root note on every change.'

It didn't matter that neither of us was an old black man from the Delta or Chicago. We were both supremely qualified to play the Blues. We were both ex-art students.

On the ground floor of the Yellow Passion Loaf's house in Kensington lived a man in hiding, a deserter from RAF training college. While on a weekend's leave, his anorexic girlfriend had turned him on to what she called the other way of flying and he'd never gone back. Because he always wore T-shirts with broad horizontal stripes we called him the Wasp, and her, the Wisp. It was their great sport to ask Ken if he wanted to smoke a joint with them.

'Only cripples need crutches,' he would say, sounding like one of the Troggs. It was peculiar: here was a guy who made Syd Barrett look like a bank clerk, yet he was straighter than a twenty-foot ruler.

From time to time I borrowed the fare money to auditions from the Wasp.

'I'm ambitious,' I intimated to him.

He looked at me with pity.

I took the money and went off with Ken to the Yodelling Sausage, a Swiss fondue house in Earls Court. We ate the disgusting stuff they served because Ken fancied the girl who sang there.

'They must've named the restaurant after her,' I said.

'Don't be such a prat.'

Soon all the money had run out and I was ready to run out with it. Tim went off to America with the ambition of going to fight in Vietnam. The last time I passed by the Yodelling Sausage it was a Kentucky Fried Chicken.

# 7

*I mean has anything weird ever happened to you? . . .*

It was a quiet night at the Speakeasy. A couple of The Who were punching each other shitless in the corner of the restaurant. I was trying to make an avocado last a couple of hours and hoping to run into someone who needed a bass player. (Must have good equipment and own transport. Dedicated. No losers, no posers. Management and record deal waiting . . . and waiting.)

A bloke called Mickey slid into the seat beside me. I'd only met him a couple of times in passing.

'Fancy doing a session tomorrow? Pye Studios, Marble Arch,' he said.

'Sure. Who's it for? What time? How much?'

'It's at seven, in the morning,' he said casually, trying to make it sound normal.

'What, is studio time cheaper at seven in the morning?'

'I suppose so. Just be there. I've got to go and round up a drummer yet.'

At chucking out time I got a cab back to World's End to pick up my guitar. I had to leave again in an hour or two so I sat in a hot bath and ate a can of tuna.

Just before seven, as I rounded the corner into Cumberland Place, I saw there was already a gaggle of musicians waiting to be led into the studios. They stood in a wide semicircle around a man who was hurling milk bottles into the air and watching

128

them smash in the middle of the road. Now he half-marched around with a jerky, erratic goose step. A rolled newspaper beneath one arm might have been a military baton. He was in his late thirties but his expression and his thinning, wild hair made him look much older. As I got nearer I saw saliva dribbling from his lower lip. His eyes stared straight ahead looking neither to the right nor the left, almost popping from their sockets. I was only a few feet away when he launched into an insane tirade. It was a private rage he screamed but it must've been heard half a mile away. A primal scream would sound like a whimper measured against this sound. The man's anger travelled through the soles of his feet. It wrenched his spine. It tore itself out beneath the root of every remaining hair and crawled all over him, turning his inside out through his bulging eyeballs and flailing limbs as he screamed his threats to the world.

I stared, open-mouthed.

Further down the street a man who stood on the pavement, washing his car, moved around to the other side of it and crouched down in the road to concentrate on a spot at the bottom of a car door. As he did so, I noticed that the mad man had two shirts on, a white one over a red one, and he wore a pair of National Health specs which he had trouble seeing through.

The producer of the session I'd turned up for – an earnest young man who looked like a student teacher – introduced himself and we shook hands. A bolt slid back and the studio doors opened behind us. The producer took hold of the mad professor by the arm and led him in.

'Who the fuck's that bloke?' I asked Mickey.

'I dunno. I've only met whassisname,' he said indicating the producer. 'He just bunged me fifty notes to get some faces together. I expect he'll bunce you up later.'

Down in the basement all the gear was set up ready for us: guitar amplifiers and a drumkit miked up, vocal mikes, with everything screened off for better sound separation. The engineer showed us to our places. A black drummer I'd never met before nodded hello and started tuning his kit. Mickey plugged in a Fender Strat that had dragons and unicorns and rainbows painted all over it. The lead guitarist began playing as all around him fuzz boxes, wah-wah pedals and echo units were clicked into life and allowed to drift further and further out of control. In the middle of the racket three backing singers huddled together for support and made futile requests to hear themselves in the headphones. Someone asked if there was a chord chart.

The producer called everyone to order.

'Aw wight,' squeaked the professor. 'Aw wight, music for the B side, play.'

There was not a sound. Sidelong glances were exchanged. Bemused expressions appeared. Shoulders were shrugged. Muttering broke out.

'Music for the B side; play. Play!'

As it began to dawn on us all that there was no music prearranged or provided, the drummer began a pedestrian four-four beat with tom-tom fills that sounded like someone tipping a pound of spuds into a cardboard box. The lead guitarist tripped over one of his foot-pedals and stumbled into a Led Zeppelin riff; Mickey and I plodded after them and the loony made a grab for the nearest mike.

'It's not on!' he shrieked.

'Put the headphones on,' the producer tried to tell him; but it was too late, the professor was already off the launch pad.

'What would you say, if you had a country and they took it away? What would you saaaaaaay?'

His eyes bulged in their sockets. Blood surged into his head and reddened his face and a lather of saliva sprayed from his lips.

'What would you say if you had a country and they took it away? Awaaaaaaaaay!!'

He ranted, oblivious to any sense of melody or rhythm.

'What would you saaaaaaaaay?!!'

There were no diminished or augmented chords in this song: solely demented ones. Then with a prehistoric yell he wrenched his tonsils through the chorus:

'Pillage and burn. Pillage and burn. Pillage, pillage and buaaaaaaaaaargh!!'

The microphone went flying but he kept pillage-and-burning. A screen went over. Then another. Finally he flung himself on the floor.

'What would you saaaaaaaaay!! Pillage!! Pillage!! And baaaaaaaaaaargggghhh!!'

He began chewing on the mike cable as he writhed on the floor. The producer signalled for us to stop and the riff dribbled away as the artiste was pulled from the floor.

'Fantastic Robin. Fantastic! Right, now let's do the A side.'

The A side was a much more commercial affair. There was a lyric sheet. There were parts for the backing singers. A video crew appeared and a cameraman wandered around recording the whole event, behaving as if he were making a documentary in Beirut. He had on a beard, a beret and a greatcoat. I bet his house was called Chez Guevara. His assistant also had a beard and followed the cameraman a yard behind, connected by an umbilical cable that ran from the power pack he was carrying in a Waitrose carrier bag with RPTV stuck on the side in electrician's tape. A third person followed these two waving a plastic windmill, but he didn't appear to be an integral part of the crew as he didn't have a beard.

'Only gong, only gong,' wailed the singers as the producer ran them through their parts.

Before I could get hold of a lyric sheet to see if I really had heard it right we set off on the riff again. Robin was being coached through his part now, and the singers echoed his words. It was a catchy little tune that moved, seemingly at r.ndom, between three notes.

*Leila the hijacker what you done wrong?*
*Let action be your only gong.*
*I can dig the skyjacker trip,*
*But if you want to stay cool, you gotta be hip.*

The music barely covered the howls of the musicians. None of us could keep a straight face any longer. Robin and his producer thought our reaction was enthusiasm, or spontaneous joy, and were driven to fresh heights of absurdity.

'Only gong, only gong . . .'

And then screens fell, mikes were tumbled again. The whole tune was polished off in one three-minute take just like the first. Robin was delighted with his performance and took a swig from a can of Coke, not noticing that it had been used as an ashtray for the whole session.

'We're all the product of the square root of minus one!' he exclaimed and ran upstairs to the control room to listen to the playback. The engineer left the tape running for him and came downstairs.

'What the fuck was all that about?'

'You know, I think it's about that Arab woman, that terrorist bird, you know, Leila ... Leila whassername, that one that they've got locked up in Ealing police station,' said Mickey. 'He must be something to do with that revolu –'

He was interrupted by a breathless youth with a red face who'd just run in.

'Have yer seen Mr Fazackerly?' he panted in an Irish accent.

'Who?'

'Mr Fazackerly! Is he here?' he said, squinting around and scratching under his pullover. 'He came into me room this morning and put me shirt on and took me glasses. I can't see a bloody thing without them, so I don't suppose he'll be able to see a bloody thing with them.'

'He's up there in the control room,' I said, pointing the way.

The squinting youth was back a minute later. 'Dere's nobody up there,' he said.

The engineer looked sick.

'Just a minute,' he said, and dashed off.

He was back quickly too. 'He's not there. He's gone. The tapes have gone. He's taken the eight-track. He hasn't paid! Where's the producer?'

The producer was gone too.

'Nobody's been paid,' I said. 'None of us.'

Faces turned toward the squinting lad.

'Now then fellers, it's nothing to do with me. He just rents the room next to mine, but he moves around all the time. He pinched me glasses –'

'Yeah, but you're the only one that knows him. Who is he?'

'I don't know. I think he used to be some sort of professor up at Oxford, a professor of maths or something. Then he – what's he call it – yeah, then he dropped out. He wrote a book about how to live with no money. He's something to do with some liberation something or other.'

I later found out that by the end of that afternoon the old bastard had ripped off a whole series of people, pressing plants and packagers, and had boxes of his record, in sleeves, out on sale by the evening.

I returned to World's End ready to nod out for a couple of hours when there was a knock on the door.

'Hello,' said the caller, a middle-aged man in a raincoat, 'I hope I'm not disturbing you but . . .' He searched for words. 'I'm a journalist. I'm writing an article about young people for a magazine and I was told I might be able to interview you,' he said.

'What's it for?' I asked.

He mumbled apologetically, trying to sound like he wasn't mumbling apologetically. 'Actually it's for *Woman's Own*.'

'What on earth do they want to know about from me?'

'It's an article about the hippie philosophy,' he said, giving the game away.

'The hippie philosophy? It's "Let it be",' I said, and closed the door.

I passed Vic on the landing. We exchanged nervous grins. He didn't speak. Ordinarily he never spoke – stayed in his room all night and all day. Wild eyed and thin as a rake he was. He slept in the clothes he always wore: black jeans and a black shirt. There were bits of white goose down, from where his mattress had burst, that stuck to his whiskers and to his hair and his clothes. No sound was ever heard coming from his room and nobody had ever been in it. The rest of us in the house tried to look after him as best we could. Sometimes if you were particularly quiet or sensitive, or stoned stupid and seeing lizards and the chariot race from

*Ben Hur* going across the ceiling, then he'd talk to you quite normally. That's when you realized what life was like for him all the time.

Vic had been a star, make no mistake about that. I'd only heard stories from people who'd seen him or worked with him but you could tell, more from the tone of voice than what was actually said, that he'd been a bit tasty.

'He was the king in France and Johnny Halliday was a feeble imitation who'd tried to fill his shoes,' they said.

'No, forget that,' they added. 'And forget Eddie Cochran. Forget, forget even Jerry Lee!'

Stories about this cat were legend. Vic had arrived at a club one night, ploughed his brand new Cadillac into a line of parked cars and then strolled in with Brigitte Bardot on his arm and ordered a bottle of champagne for everyone in the place. By now he looked like a phantom but you could picture how it must have been. He was still a good-looking man, fifteen years out of date and, so it turns out, twenty years ahead of his time. Fuelled with amphetamine and in a black leather suit he used to tear concert halls apart. Nobody, but nobody, would follow him onstage. Then one night before a concert he climbed into his suit, greased back his hair and swallowed a handful of pills. But the era of innocence was passing: a lot of wonderful and weird new chemicals were about. A couple of decades earlier, the Sandoz laboratories had succeeded in synthesizing a chemical for possible use in treating the hallucinations and problems of schizophrenia. It was called d-lysergic acid diethylamide 25. Nobody knew how the mistake happened that night, but instead of swallowing a few leapers to help him rock out, without knowing it he swallowed a few tabs of acid.

He locked himself in a cupboard for three days.

When he went onstage again, he was dressed in white, and blessed the audience. Then he had his flat replumbed so that when the cooker was turned on a fountain of water came from the gas ring.

I knew Vic only as a silent and timid man, who always looked as if he were lost. The last time I saw him was in the car park of Newport Pagnell services. I was coming back from a gig. He was hitching up to Coventry to see his mum. There was a brown paper carrier bag in his hand. He opened it to show me the tiny kitten inside.

# 8

On the road things are laid out end to end. For the traveller there are all kinds of other connections that are made across time. But time had somehow diminished what I was looking for. All that was left were the kind of tales like these by which a man likes to define himself. Deeper inside me something had been crossed and recrossed many times by a shadow. This shadow had taken the silver thread of remembering and woven it into a net that had caught me fast. This was the net of things learnt: the network of opinions and judgements about this, that and everybody. Now I realized that it wasn't so much that I held all these memories, but that they held me. These reminiscences crept into every day and led me through the same events time after time, round and round in circles. For the last hundred miles I'd sat silently repeating them to myself. (The driver had heard them all before and more than once.) Now there was no mileage left in them. Not even to get me to the next hotel.

All those other days simply led back here. It was the past that decided how I felt. When it rained I was miserable. When I read a newspaper I grew angry. Nothing new would ever find a way in through this web-like armour of privacy, criticism, envy and regret.

Though scratching a good living from the armpit of modern culture might be called something of a luxury, I could no longer deny the instinct that my life was passing me by unlived. It was something that couldn't be left alone. Like the tooth here, with the missing piece, that the end of my tongue kept probing: I kept pushing at it simply because it was right here in me.

The day had stirred new feelings that couldn't be arranged in any customary or time-proven order. I'd simply run out of tricks that worked. This feeling would not be bought off with a stolen joke, a flip one-liner or another anecdote.

That funeral procession of trucks which had been passing alongside all day: I knew who it was for.

I stared out through the windscreen, but saw only the white line stretching ahead and my own face staring back at me, a reflection lit from below and the left by the lights in the dashboard instruments. The blobby headlights of cars and trucks approaching from the opposite direction turned all the raindrops on the window into hundreds of little beacons. Up ahead a neon sign twisted, turning them red blue green, red blue green. I laughed out loud when I saw that the sign read simply BEER PIZZA GAS.

We pulled in.

Boisterous and animated conversation broke out as people emerged, puffy eyed and arthritic, from Jonestown, with complexions the healthy colour of a docker's vest. The Drummer was being led along by the Keyboard Player. Apparently, as they'd become more and more pissed, the Drummer had passed out on his back. The Keyboard Player had balanced the pepper for the Bloody Marys on the Drummer's nose, hoping to make him sneeze as he slept. Unhappily, the lark had turned to a linnet and, when the pepper toppled, instead of falling into the Drummer's nostrils, it fell right into his eyes and had left him unable to see for the past two hours.

'A case of the blind drunk leading the blind,' I sniffed haughtily.

We went in to the truckstop. There was a shop and a
restaurant, both defiantly free of charm. The aisles in the shop
were narrow and I had to walk slowly behind a woman who
was too fat to walk properly. On sale were cheap cowboy
shirts and boots, belt-buckles and postcards. One of the cards
showed that near by, where the old Route 66 goes through
Amarillo, a helium magnate had lined up ten classic Cadillacs
and half-buried them, nose down in the ground, with their fins
sticking up in the air. Here, even this could be regarded as an
improvement of the landscape. Another was a 'Wildlife of the
Desert' postcard showing a Roadrunner. Beep beep.

In the restaurant I sat at one of the long counters. The menu
was displayed on the wall. A large box lit from the inside, it
had photographs of the meals on offer, five times bigger than
life-size. The colours had gradually faded leaving only the bluer
tones. The blue frankfurters looked the least appetizing. There
were neon beer signs; there were Cowboys and Broncos football pennants, showing that this really was a half-way house,
and there was a display of Moo Cow Creamers: milk jugs
shaped like standing cows that poured the milk from their
mouths! You could buy one if you asked the waitress.

We sat alongside men in ventilated nylon baseball hats, the
kind that told you what beer their owners drank. It had been
a while since any of these guys had played baseball. Here they
served food to fill pot-bellies. There were piles of cotton-
wool bread rolls and tubs of whipped-up butter, beef, mash
and cabbage in separate bowls along with dull-looking beetroot. The women here wore lemon, lilac and turquoise tops,
and spray-on jeans. They were much too skinny or far too
fat.

The waitress had a face assembled from parboiled potatoes,

orchid-coloured lipstick and a perfume that would ground a
swarm of tsetse flies. Round her neck she wore a gold chain
with her name – Della – and she looked like the kind of
woman who could kick-start a 747. She put her arm up behind
her back to scratch, as if she were winding herself up, then as
she turned I could see that she was buffing up her engagement
ring. It was nice to see that someone could be so vacant *and*
engaged at the same time. It promised to be neither rewarding
nor pleasant to disturb her but it made a welcome change from
being told to 'have a nice day'. I waited while she put some
coins in the jukebox, then she came over and took my order,
raising her notebook as if she were a referee booking me for a
particularly nasty foul.

Here was my punishment – on the jukebox – a mawkish,
soporific song straight from the heart of popcorn Country:
music so weak it could barely stagger from the speakers.
Records like this were knocked out in Nashville quicker than
the truckstop's blue frankfurters. The songs dealt with all the
possible permutations of leaving and returning, but despite all
the different emotions that the lyrics claimed were involved,
the voices always had a strange, whining flatness to them,
broken up here and there with a few vocal tricks:

> *When I die I may not get to heaven,*
> *'cos I'm not sure that they let cowboys in,*
> *Well if they don't, then let me go to Texas,*
> *'cos Texas is the best place that I've bin.*

(The Drummer had a theory about why country music
seems to have only three tempos: When the early settlers made
their way south and west it was in a wagon or on horseback;
there were horses that went fast and there were horses that

went slow; and there was a horse with a gimpy leg that went along in three-four time.)

Above the tedious and maudlin sentiments that were being endlessly repeated, and above the treacle strings and the wheezing, senile pedal-steel and the plip-plopping of the bass there was the counterpoint of punters playing on fruit machines and video games.

'What you got there?'

I turned to face the man who'd sat down beside me. He had a soft, pale face that was accentuated by the clear plastic spectacles that he wore: the Milky Bar Kid had come of age. He'd noticed that I was about to pay with the pound note. I handed it to him. It certainly appeared strange to him. He turned it over several times without comment while a perplexed frown settled into his features.

'English money,' I said.

'English money,' he repeated and thought a while longer. 'How many hamburgers would this get me?'

'It's worth about two dollars,' I said.

'I . . . suppose . . . then . . .' (This guy didn't continue to speak. He started each word separately and eventually they were strung into a sentence. He gave the impression of a heavy goods train lurching slowly forward.) 'I suppose then,' he began again, 'that if I went to England I'd have to change my American money into English money . . .'

'That's right.'

'. . . if I wanted to buy a hamburger or a cup o' coffee,' he finished.

'Yes.'

'I suppose I'd have to do that at a bank, would I?' he asked in all seriousness.

'Yes,' I added again, as matter-of-factly as I could: anybody as viciously stupid as this might have been dangerous.

It was one of those days: there are days when you get on a tube or a bus and step straight into a Hieronymus Bosch painting where everyone has a leer or a squint, or seems somehow distorted and strange.

'You drive a truck?' I ventured.

'No sir, I work in the Burden Ham.'

'The Burden Ham, what's that?'

'No, the Burdin Han. It's a restaurant, up the road apiece.'

Now it was my turn to appear stupid. 'Oh you mean the Bird-in-Hand Restaurant,' I said, as if I'd explained the mystery to him.

'Yeah, that's what I said.'

'But don't you get free meals up there?' I said, indicating the big piece of pie that Della had placed next to his coffee.

'I sure do, but I got two hours to kill 'til I get my ride up to Mount Joy.'

'What's Mount Joy?' I said, unable to make any phonetic variations on that.

'Where I live.'

'Is that near here?' I said to keep things moving.

'Thirty-five miles.'

'What time do you get home then?'

'Ten o'clock.'

'Then what time do you have to leave in the morning?'

'I get me a ride in at six.'

'But that means you only get eight hours a day at home, what do you get time to do there?' I said.

'Sleep.'

'Is Mount Joy a big place?' I said.

'Sure is. Five thousand people, near enough.'

It was hard to see how there could be a Mount anything around these parts and by the sound of it he lived somewhere about as joyful as it was hilly.

He turned to face me directly. The face was so blank and the eyes, small and staring as if he'd spent too many years on a video game, made me feel uncomfortable.

'You look unhappy,' he said, taking me aback. 'Perhaps I might help.'

My resentment was lessened by the impotence and the lack of threat that I read in his face.

'I'm not unhappy for me, mate, only for the state of the world,' I lied.

His hand reached slightly towards me. He smelt a convert. 'I knew I must speak to you,' he said. 'I could see that your heart is troubled.'

'Save me from being saved,' I found myself saying inwardly as he recounted the various stages of his own conversion while I looked aloof from the corner of my eye.

When I began to move impatiently he gripped my arm tighter, and ignoring my face he searched my eyes for the consent that would allow him to shove me tottering to the brink of salvation. Avoiding his gaze I looked across the restaurant and watched a truck driver shove coin after coin into a slot. He did this so passively that it appeared that they were part of the same mechanism and the machine was playing him just as much. Reach, drop, jingle. Pull, spin, click.

A row of video games lined up against a wall flashed out the challenge: YOU ARE THE SOLE HOPE FOR THE SURVIVAL OF THE HUMAN RACE.

Could I take all that responsibility? I looked around me, and listened. I loved 'the human race'. It was just its individual members that I found hard to bear. Would I ever be fearless enough to accept everyone as they are? Let alone love them.

The man mistook my gaze. 'I believe you are seeing. The spirit is moving in you.' He glanced upwards for emphasis but seemed not to notice that above him was a rotating fan that said 'Wild Turkey' on the blades.

I couldn't answer, either with word or gesture. Again, he mistook my long silence.

'My friend, I believe you are coming through.'

But as the grip on my arm tightened I stiffened and his hand retreated.

We sat – the Milky Bar Kid and me – like two biped insects on a great ball in space, making feeble sounds from time to time, both of us believing that we were on to the truth. It was as ridiculous, as someone once said, as two fleas arguing about who owns the dog they're living on. I decided that I had to get outside.

The driver had swallowed a quick cup of coffee and driven the bus over to some pumps to be refuelled. At three miles to the gallon, the fuel tanks on the bus needed to hold more than a hundred gallons. It would take several minutes to fill them, while the tyres had their regular check.

The air outside wasn't the spicy, perfumed mix of mountain country and the South that it can be. The rain had rinsed all that away. Every minute or so a truck hissed wetly down the road. The three gas pumps, which stood opposite a workshop, looked as if they'd been lifted from an Edward Hopper painting.

From the workshop came the sound of the brothers getting funky. I picked my way between deep puddles with oil swirls in them and poked my nose around the door of the workshop. The mechanics didn't notice me as they danced and pratted about while a ghetto-blaster the size of a suitcase played beat-box music. It occurred to me that the mechanical tune which held their attention didn't sound half as much like music as a well-tuned engine.

The night was thick and obscure. There were stars out but the light from the restaurant made them difficult to see, so I walked away, passing between a row of trucks with tyres four feet high. Their engines had been left running to keep the generators turning and their refrigeration units working. Even in the belting rain I was glad to be out and able to walk around. Then I saw a fat woman leaving the truck stop, waddling as fast as she could and dumping herself into the front seat of a large car, making it wallow.

I wondered if I was 'walking properly', or rather, if there was a better way. For a while I walked around with longer steps. Then I tried short quick steps, watching my feet as they landed on the wet ground. First I turned my toes in, and then out. I stamped along splashing with flat and heavy feet, then crept as lightly as I could to leave no trace of my ever having been there, thinking how clever I was exactly to match the movements of my long, shivering shadow. I tried to move like a cat whose muscles are unbroken by useless contractions – as if 'trying' were the right way to do it. I enjoyed being deliberately aware of my weight shifting as my feet moved across the ground. There was a great satisfaction in just walking, in just letting the movement take place without trying to do it. It was movement without ambition and without inhibition. It was a true sensation.

'How do you tell the dancer from the dance?' asked the poet.

*145*

I and the movement were indeed one process. It felt almost as if time had become biological. It existed only for itself as changing movement.

I stopped and looked up at a handful of stars that were bright enough to cut through the night. Then I realized again that of course they were already somewhere else, or gone. I was looking light-years into, and genuinely seeing, the past. Their light had taken so long to reach me that some of them must be showing where they actually were when I was a boy. My past was present: if I could see deeply enough, then perhaps I would see a place where all time is present. I felt myself to be like a fragment of a hologram that, however vaguely, held in fuzzy detail the whole image of creation.

All the feelings that the day had stirred up – all the ghostly processes and inner voices – were all quite in keeping. They were neither intruders nor strangers. They belonged neither to night or day, nor to the past, present or future. They were here and everywhere else at once, as old as time, as fresh as the moment.

It isn't time that moves clocks: that's done by cogs and springs. For a minute I had nowhere to go to, just as the stars above me had no *where* that they were going to. I stamped around in the puddles and the muck grunting to myself so that I was at last forced to start laughing. 'But a pig don't need no time!'

Like a snake, another long truck passed with its eighteen big tyres hissing at me.

Then I heard my name being called.

# 9

It had remained dark all day and a black tarpaulin had gradually been dragged across the sky. The rain drove against the windscreen faster than the wipers could shift it. Our headlights cut only fifty feet into the slanting rain. While the engine in the back droned to itself, up front the silence had a voice of its own.

Mile after mile, mile after mile went by.

An hour later it was still raining and an hour after that there was no change. Water had collected in the places where the highway was uneven making the big bus roll and splash like a ship at sea. When there was a rise in the road, the drone of the engine became heavier. Then as the road levelled out, it fell away until the deep swell began again. As the engine churned on, oblivious to everything except its own internal rhythms, so I sat and became absorbed in my own internal rhythms and the mechanisms of my own body.

In the foremost compartment of the ship all the rising and falling was felt in the stomach. I sensed the rise and fall of my own solar plexus itself as life was breathed into me. I could almost sense the blood circulating round and round inside me. Then, when I squeezed my eyes tight I saw intricate patterns: glassy-bright arabesques and spirals, appearing out of the blood-purple depths. Thoughts, and then the feelings that followed them bringing expressions to my face, swam through me like fish. Lazy at one moment, suddenly they darted this way and that, never resting completely. I stared at the soft pink shape near to me and saw, in an uninvolved sort of way, that it was a hand. Somehow not my hand, it lived its own life: a fleshy starfish free to drift and float. The pink starfish, my hand, rested now on the blue of my coat – the blue becoming deep and vivid. I watched over the hand now, attentive to its gentle stillness in the swimming, swarming world. Slowly this calm seeped into my arm. Slowly, slowly, gently, it flowed through me, stilling all the frantic activity in me that I'd not previously been aware of. First all the fluttering on the surface began to settle, then the calmness moved deeper and deeper, releasing each layer of muscular tension, until nothing moved but the flow of this awareness, my breathing (which gradually slowed down) and the beating of my heart. This new awareness in the body began to free me from the thousand forces that usually dominated my thought and feeling and, though this peace was threatened on all sides, little by little a fragile order was established.

In the Middle Ages when a journey to the end of the world was undertaken, people believed that at a certain point they must reach the edge and fall into the unknown. But when a brave man or a fool held to a straight course, after some strange experiences and with some effort, he sailed on until he came to the place he'd set out from. In this way it was discovered that the world is round and that in reality the traveller's straight course is a circle.

I knew the world was round: I'd already been round it three times. But I found that I kept returning to the same events, and to the same feelings and the same ideas. I was beginning to see that time is circular and that for some reason my travels were trying to lead me back to the origin.

My strange craft was being invited nearer and nearer towards an island shore. There was no flag here, nor any other piece of coloured rag flapping from a pole to show my ownership. Anyway, this place certainly didn't belong to me. Rather, it was I who belonged to this place.

This was the island where I'd stolen time from school and spent it on myself. This island had become whatever I'd wanted. I had come here nearly every day until (at what point I can't exactly say) I began, at times, to notice a strange separation in myself. While the one part of me continued to drift and dream, inventing more and more extravagant adventures, another part was able to see these dreams taking shape without being completely lost to them.

My first dreams were the dreams of a child who charged into imaginary fights, not on a horseback, but on the footplate of an A4-class Pacific locomotive: it was as easy as riding a bike. I wasn't much older when women appeared, who were always finding excuses to take off their costumes to perform better the roles I'd arranged for them. The playful dreams became curious, amusing and then wet, as they were able to search out more and more of my imagination to feed on. It was here also that I was smothered by dark beauties who pleaded with me to possess them again, but on this occasion I paused instead to paint an erotic masterpiece, the cool and detached eye of the artist noting the ecstatic expressions that my powers had coaxed on to their faces as they lay half-asleep in the sand, the short black curls flattened and matted by the motions and moistures of our meeting while, like an exotic fruit that could no longer contain its passion, the pink lips, gorgeous and engorged, slowly leaked the secret, sticky transparency that had completed the almost magical transference of the milky and musky fluids from each of us to the other.

The fantastic became ever more fantastic as it found each new disguise.

Later the island became a kind of ideal state where no poverty, or cruelty, or crime existed. Art was pursued and nature enjoyed under clear blue skies and perpetual sunshine. It was here on this island, for instance, that I granted audience to men who had travelled far to see me, and where I would humbly accept the homage that was due to a revered Blues Guitar King.

But I could no longer put ashore here and lose myself in romance. Romance was no longer something wild and dark. It wasn't cold and deep like an ocean. This place I was approaching had the look of a sleepy haven, wet and green, that was lapped by a safe and shallow sea.

I wanted one last, long look at this lost world of my younger days. From this distance they seemed so light and easy. But were they really like that? I peered closer, straining to see, until I could focus clearly on one week in particular . . .

. . Earlier than usual in the school holidays the restlessness had set in. During the first week I'd bent the front forks of my bike so badly that they couldn't be repaired. Just outside the village where we lived there was a wood with a network of cycle tracks that wound through the trees and across deeper and deeper gullies. Feeling compelled to try and outdo my mates, I'd gone flying at one of these chasms, dropping down over one side and pedalling flat-out so that the momentum would take me up the other side. But I'd hit a patch of wet leaves at the bottom and skidded into a tree.

The day before I'd cycled the three miles into Stockton-on-Tees to meet my grandma and grandad off their train from Nottingham. They were to spend two weeks with us and I was there so that I could show them to the new bus stop, now that the changed one-way system had altered the layout of the High Street. My dad hadn't been able to collect them in our car because he was on the wrong shift. The train was due early in the morning but I'd arrived even earlier and spent an unbroken hour simply staring into the window of the Hamilton's music shop at the first American electric guitar to arrive in Stockton: a flame red Fender Stratocaster, exactly the same as the one I'd seen Hank Marvin with when I'd been forced to sit through Cliff Richard in *Babes in the Wood* so that I could see The Shadows play 'Apache' at the Globe the previous Christmas.

Now I had no bike. The grown-ups spent all the time talking. They were off, miles away in the past, where no one could reach them.

I spent a morning in the garage making a guitar from my cricket bat and the strings I'd taken from my dad's old violin. Because I could only get one note out of it, I sawed it into the crude shape of a machine gun only to have dad take it off me and break it in half when he had seen what I'd done.

'You've had your birthday so don't think you'll be getting another one because you won't.'

'That's all right; I wanted a tennis racket anyway.'

'If I'd have talked like that to my mother, she'd have wiped the floor with my face,' said my grandma.

And there was more trouble that day. On my way from the corner shop I'd squirted the little girl from next door with one of those yellow plastic lemons full of juice. It had made her eyes sting and made her cry. I couldn't stand her: her bright ginger hair and the way she was always sucking her thumb, with her other hand always in her knickers. Her mother came to see mine to make sure that I didn't get away with it. So I smeared over next-door's garage windows with revenge-coloured paint; an hour later I was cleaning it all off with a rag and a jam jar full of petrol.

'Any more out of you and I'll clatter you.'

'He's only doing it to show off,' said my grandma.

That Sunday there was yet more trouble when the vicar from the local Methodist Church approached my mother to ask, discreetly, if everything was all right at home and why I hadn't put any money in the collection plate for some weeks. But I hadn't been keeping it to spend; just before I arrived at Sunday School I would plop the pennies down a drain so that I could be independent with a clean conscience.

It was my friend 'Mub' Lloyd who showed me how to make a weed-killer and sugar bomb by packing a length of copper piping with a mixture of their crystals. With a hammer and a nail, a small hole was opened in the middle of the pipe, then the ends were flattened out and crimped over tight. Both operations were potentially lethal. The bomb was then put in place with a trail of the powder acting as a fuse. Over in the old quarry we blew a concrete fence post clean out of the ground. Then it was my turn to go and get some more supplies.

'– oh, and a tin of Sodium Chlorate, please.'

'What d'you want that for?'

'It's for my dad. He said it's to get the weeds on the garden path.'

'You've only got a little garden.'

'It's for our allotment.'

For a while we blew up dustbins. Sometimes they would glow white-hot and disintegrate, and sometimes there was a bang that would rattle every window in the street. Then we began to experiment. A rocket made of tubing failed to take off but when, after several minutes' wait and after we approached it and I picked it up, it began to fizz, we covered a hundred yards in a flash and then we were sick.

It was time for me to keep my head down. There was talk around the village tea-tables about how a series of explosions had sent Copper Earle out to Trotter's Farm to check their shotgun licence. So I stayed in my bedroom and read about the Hole in the Wall Gang in the *Pictorial History of the Wild West*. Or I painted.

I began a painting of some roses, which gradually looked less and less like roses and became more and more abstract; when it ended up looking like a giant red claw in a churned-up field I signed it, and entitled it *War* and presented it to my grandma.

Or I sat in the garage in the old Austin Ruby, and went everywhere without moving. Or I simply sat and watched the sunlight filtering through the dust in the air.

'Come out of there, you'll strain the steering.'

'I'm only moving my hands, not the steering wheel.'

Then came the day we went to the seaside. The women were making sandwiches: one lot of corned beef, minced onion and tomato – a mixture that turns the bread into an instant sog – and a batch made with beetroot from the allotment that stained deep magenta patches on the white slices.

'Can't we have banana sandwiches, Mam?'

'No.'

'Aw, why not?'

'Because we haven't got any bananas.'

'Yes, we have no bananas –' my dad began singing.

'Give over, Fred!'

I was sent back upstairs to get changed again.

'But why can't I wear jeans?'

'Because you're not going out in a two-bob top with a tuppenny-ha'penny bottom.'

We set off for the station: the car was too small to take us all to the seaside. To reach the station we had to walk through the dangerous territory where neighbours *thought*. This was where we had to behave – 'or else the neighbours'll *think* we can't bring you up right'.

The train took us past Middlesbrough's only landmark, the Transporter Bridge, where a whole section of road is swung on thick steel cables across the River Tees to South Bank; though even this dubious claim to fame has to be shared with an identical bridge in Runcorn. We went through Dorman Long's steelworks where, as parents never tired of telling you, they'd made the girders for the Sydney Harbour Bridge. For miles afterwards the railway was flanked on either side by Imperial Chemical Industries where sulphur dioxide is pumped out to rot the curtains and kill the window boxes of Teesside.

A sad sun burned blood-red through the thick, chemical haze as we passed fields of caravans and one where fourteen houses were going up, to be sold for £4,500 each. As we clattered past a wooden platform called Warrenby Halt, I kept a look out through the acid sky for the tall chimney that, even in the day, burned with a bright flame.

Saltburn is a late Victorian seaside resort with an air of genteel decay. There are a few miles of sand and woods that cut inland up narrow valleys. It has a short pier, a cliff railway and a little fun-fair with swings and roundabouts, miniature golf and a boating lake. Running along the cliff top is a row of guest houses and, like an over-ornate bookend at the edge of the cliffs, there is a posh hotel: The Zetland. The town was purpose built as a resort for the nouveaux riches, the captains of the ironstone industry, and the railway had run there since 1862. Now there is no railway and half the pier has been taken away; the other half has been left for the unemployed to pass their days, and nights, fishing.

When I was a boy, Saltburn had come to rely on day-trippers who went the extra three stops past Redcar because Redcar was 'common'. Redcar got all the crowds from Middlesbrough; they called those that stayed on the train 'a snobby lot'.

Saltburn was never really busy. More often than not there was a mist of cold sea-spray but on the day that I went with my grandparents the beach was bathed in sunshine. That year there was an Indian summer, an unusual heatwave whose sweetness even the wind that always blows along the North-East coast couldn't remove.

When older people were with us we didn't have to walk all the way down the cliff paths and steps to get on the Prom. Instead, we took the cliff railway and then walked along the Prom towards the Cliff End, away from the mouth of the Tees where there was always a smell suspiciously like shit.

We wandered up and down the beach looking at 'spots' until we found a spot by the pier. The beach was free of pebbles but there was a thin layer of sea coal left behind by the sea; when we'd all gone home local people would come and scrape it up into bags. A cluster of rowing boats and tractors with tarpaulins over them would shelter us if the breeze got up too strong.

My grandma sat and, with her legs straight out in front of her, ate a Penguin. A dog came all the way from the sea before it shook itself dry all over a shrieking family on another nearby spot. My mother took some snaps with the box Brownie which would (as usually happened when we got the prints back from the chemist) have everyone disappearing off the left-hand edge.

I walked beneath the pier which had girders with star shapes cut out of them. Mussels clung to its legs and where they left off fern-like seaweed hung from its cross-braces. It looked like an underwater theatre. A man dug for fishing bait around one of the pier legs and whenever he found a sand eel he cut it up with a pair of nail scissors and put it in an Oxo tin.

I helped my sister make a sandcastle. She was usually so quiet that this is the first clear memory of her that arises from that day. We piled up a mound of sand, shaped the walls and towers, and then dug out a deep moat and a long canal down the beach, ready for when the tide came in to fill it. Five minutes later a boy came over and stamped the banks of our canal flat and filled in a short section of it. He was working for the man who was in competition with the donkey rides and who took children on short rides up and down the beach. He had a short train: two silly open carriages that ran on little rubber tyres pulled behind a tractor which had flat wooden panels that had been cut out and painted to look like a railway engine. At the front the train had a grinning face. It looked ridiculous.

I ran up behind the boy and, without stopping, in one movement I leaped through the air and brought my spade swinging down across his backside with a stinging crack, landed, and kept running all the way back to our spot where I was safe. The boy ran after me, and stood trembling while I stood casually behind my mother. The boy's eyes were welling with tears: I'd hurt him. He was so hurt he didn't even want to retaliate.

'It's all right luv, I saw what he did. He's going to come round here and say sorry,' she said.

'Little sod,' added my grandma.

When we were kids we didn't know that she was in almost constant pain as a result of being knocked down by a taxi in Bradford. Now, when I look at the old photographs, I notice that it's a brave smile and there is still a twinkle in her eye.

When it came to twelve o'clock the bags were unpacked to eat. One of the thermos flasks poured out a stream of cold tea and broken glass into the plastic top that was used as a cup. Sandwiches were handed round.

'Mam, are they called sandwiches because they always have sand in them?'

Of course they weren't.

Then my sister and I played at being sand witches. Then sad witches.

I was sent to get some ice-creams. The stall that sold the ice-cream sold lots of other things as well: seaside rock, plastic windmills, postcards with jokes I couldn't understand, and souvenirs. I counted up the pocket money I had left. If I bought the cheapest ice-creams on the stall, didn't have one myself, and added the money that had been saved to my pocket money, then I'd have just enough to buy a penknife! I took the ice-creams back and handed them round.

'Where's yours?'

'I ate it on the way back.'

I strolled off under the pier and took the penknife out of my pocket. It was a cheap souvenir penknife that must have been sitting on the stall for some time. There were little specks of rust appearing on the metal and the side panels had a fading colour photo of the pier, whose clear plastic covering was beginning to peel away. I struggled to open the blade and then prised a mussel from one of the pier legs. Then I practised throwing the knife so that it would stick in the sand. But I couldn't close the knife: the blade had stuck open. I made a big effort and the blade snapped shut, across my finger, cutting deep into it and trapping it at the same time. I walked back to our spot and held out my hand.

My dad bent the blade back and a hanky was wrapped around the bleeding wound while people turned out their bags looking for a plaster.

'I knew he was up to something,' said my grandma.

There were no plasters in anyone's handbag and the cut wouldn't stop bleeding so my dad marched me along to Boots the Chemists in the High Street, pulling me along by the arm so that when we got there I felt dizzy.

'It should really have a stitch put in it,' said the man in a white coat as he put something on the cut that made it sting and then bandaged it up. I couldn't understand why he was being nicer than my father and why he touched my finger so carefully.

We packed up and moved off. My sister and I had our photograph taken while we sat on the back of a little horse. It was all that was left of an old roundabout that lay in pieces around it. When we went round the fun-fair, my sister went on the rides for being good.

'I'll just stand and watch the dodgems, Mam.'

'Well just make sure you do.'

Then suddenly an electric racket cut through the atmosphere of the day like a blowtorch: it was not the noise of the clashing cars, but a monkey screaming 'Gonna tell Aunt Mary 'bout Uncle John!'

'What's that record, Mister?' I asked the bloke with the long greasy hair at the pay booth.

'Little Richard, son.'

This was a message from another planet. How could anything so dumb be so exciting? I'd been touched.

The sound submerged as we walked along the beach and up through the ornamental gardens, where flowers were lined up in neat, box-edged beds, and down into one of those valleys where stunted trees leaned against the prevailing wind. The walls of the ravine rose steeply. High above, it was crossed by a spindly, iron bridge. The path threaded through wild grass and banks of stinging-nettles and thin saplings with tendrils of shining ivy. A cloud of midges danced over the surface of the brook that ran along the bottom beside the track of the miniature railway. It was hazy and humid, dappled in light and shade. Bees droned louder than birds sang, as they struggled, sap-laden, through air so thick and sticky with a honeyed light of its own that they seemed to be swimming rather than flying. The heavy scent of wild garlic was gradually replaced with something even wilder: the smell of a real locomotive.

At the start of the railway line there was a ticket office and a turnstile, even though the low platform had no fence around it. A hundred yards along the track there was a short tube where corrugated-iron sheets had been bent over to make a tunnel. It was only a miniature railway, but I was only a miniature person. The ordinary train that had brought us to the seaside this morning was too big, like a house. This was a *real* locomotive: bigger than me! It had maroon livery, lined in black and gold, and it had a spirit, an aura of white steam of its own making. It was a real loco because it had its name on a shiny brass plate arched over the middle driving wheel.

There were no passengers on the platform: they weren't taking any more rides. It was the end of the day and everyone was going home. The family sat down to rest their feet, saying they'd nearly walked their legs off. My grandad was talking to the driver. My grandad was an engine driver himself, but he didn't drive expresses; he only drove excursion trains that didn't have names. The heat of the day was still in the air but the heat from the loco was intense. Everything was quiet, as if even the sounds around were consumed in the heat. The whole of me wished for something with an intensity that equalled it. The almost deliberate suffering of that moment was in not knowing what I was wishing for. But whatever it was, it first meant that I should climb on to the footplate of the locomotive.

I stepped on. Above the boiler the heat haze made the track ahead shimmer and vibrate with life – life stretching out ahead. Magic. I looked over the brass levers and the glass gauges and –

'Bloody hell, kid, get off there!'

The driver had screamed as loud as he did to frighten me. And so it did, for years.

I don't think I wanted to take the train anywhere in particular. What I really wanted didn't lie in the future, down the line, any more than it lies now in conjuring up colourful memories, or in colouring memories to try and paint a more interesting picture. What did I want? Perhaps it was simply a wish to be – standing there in that spot with all its possibilities intact.

Sitting on the tour bus, I recalled the feeling of how every Christmas Eve, when all the presents were laid out under the branches of the tree they could still be anything. Early on Christmas morning when we would get up, shivering, to open them, there would always be something for my train set from my grandad, something like a signal box. It was never a Little Richard record, or a proper penknife. My childhood was neither as simple and innocent, nor as legendary and mysterious, as I am pleased to pretend it was. These weren't light and easy days. They'd been difficult days full of disappointment and doubt.

# 10

I once went to Southwold in reply to a small ad in *Classic & Thoroughbred Car* magazine. Southwold turned out to be exactly the kind of retirement ghetto where a doctor's widow would put her late husband's Jaguar up for sale. The car, a Mk II 3·8 finished in metallic golden sand, had done less than two hundred miles a week; it had a leather and walnut interior and was half the price of a brand-new, Euro-moulded clone-mobile.

I'd seen the Jag and driven it. Whoever said that smell is the most evocative of the senses was right. Basking, bathing in nostalgia, the aroma of the car's interior took me straight back to the days of family outings to the coast, even though we had a somewhat humbler old Austin. The Jaguar was sprightly, but it belonged to a different era and in all honesty it wasn't as much fun as a GTi that could be hurled around corners. The Jag would have taken twice as long to get back to London as the car I'd arrived in, though what I'd do with the time saved was open to question: having decided not to buy the car, I had a day to spend instead.

I parked in the middle of the village. In a tea-shop window a semicircle of gingerbread men were propped in static dance around a plate of maids of honour. Inside I ordered at the counter where a hand-lettered notice read, 'Credit will only be given to persons over 85 years of age if accompanied by both parents'.

I took a table by the window so that I was able to see both

outside and inside. A radio, piped through to a small loud-speaker in the corner above me, played safe, old songs and the mock-jolly, oom-pah melodies that accompany Spanish holidays and sound like watered-down drinking songs. A lady at the adjacent table sat alone, sipped milky coffee and read *The Lady*.

Two silver-haired old soldiers came in. They were dressed similarly in cavalry twill, check and tweed, and as they took a table they made a painstaking ritual of placing their carrier bags with neatly folded raincoat and cap beside the table. (Ready for inspection, sir!) That done, they were able to continue the conversation they'd been holding as they came in. It appeared that some local punks had ripped up a flower bed:

'They don't give a damn, do they?'

'No, they don't care tuppence.'

On the radio John Fred and his Playboy Band played and sang the old hit, 'Judy in Disguise (with Glasses)'. The throbbing bass guitar that once would have caused winces of pain and anguish in the older generation went unnoticed, now accepted as part of the vocabulary of modern life, like floppy disks and litter. The news headlines announced a bad plane crash somewhere in the Alps, the cause of which would be probably determined as soon as the rescue party had discovered the famously indestructible 'black box', which would have a record of the events leading up to the crash. Had nobody ever thought of building the planes themselves out of the same material as the box? Then followed an untypically bad piece of PR coordination: the Prime Minister was heard urging young people to be 'more adult', to stay at home and not become 'drifters', while close on her heels the Chairman of the party demanded that they get on their bikes and go looking for work.

A jolly-hockey-sticks kind of gell sang about how many kinds of sweet flowers grow in an English Country Garden in a voice syrupy and cloying enough to spread on the toasted teacake which had just been placed in front of me.

Sitting with her back to me, a woman helped an older man with his sandwich. His pained expression reflected his puzzlement with the world, and, as he looked over, with me. My first reaction was to retreat inside or turn away; I tried not to smile a patronizing smile but simply to hold my gaze, steady and impartial.

I left the tea shop and walked towards the sea, alongside a row of Regency houses with their filigree ironwork – houses that were big enough to turn into hotels, as some had been. A small, public garden was being restocked with new blooms. The damaged flowers had been raked to one side while plants fresh from the nursery were being dropped into the ground in their place.

The window display in the Co-op announced a 24-hour Personal Funeral Service. Presumably anyone not taking advantage of the Co-op's offer had to die at a more convenient time. A black marble headstone was ready-carved: 'In Loving Memory'. Underneath there was a blank area for the details to be filled in. I stared at it for a short while, picturing the obvious.

The tides scoured the crumbly headlands pulling at the sand and shingle and, just like a bather lowering himself into a chilly sea, so the east coast appeared to be edging itself into the cold brown water. Even the lighthouse at Southwold, built at the end of the last century, had been built in someone's back garden. Had it been built in the obvious place, on the low cliff edge, it would have crumbled into the sea long ago. Every pebble underfoot had been washed here from further north.

Down by the sea was a strip of firm sand where I could walk. I began to drift south, away from the cluster of snug and smug retirement villas, painted off-white and cream in pale contentment where people come and go within well-defined limits like the labradors and spaniels on their elasticated leads.

'Lovely day.'

Soon I was walking across the marshes, past the scuffed and bashed-up fishing boats and the piles of dredged-up mud, through the sparse, blue smoke of a bonfire, past the Ebb Tide Mobile Disco, a broken wind pump, and past a gaudy, wooden hut where a couple were taking their lunch from tupperware containers while a kettle sighed on a gas ring.

I carried on through the dunes to the edge of the sea, crunching through the pebbles and sounding like a crisp-eating castanet player.

Soon I was passing the remains of Dunwich, a melancholy village that five centuries ago boasted a harbour of dozens of ships and a daily market. The town had been slowly clawed away by the sea until the last remaining church had collapsed on the beach in 1920.

At the end of the long curve of coast, a mile away, stood the great, utilitarian block of Sizewell nuclear power station, black against the sky. It had been the only visible point of reference in this shifting, sifting day. A mile away, I could already hear the whirring and the hum. Although it was growing dark, everything had an acid colour. The gorse looked pale and bleached like the ill-white grass. Two scuffed and bashed-up fishermen drew their boat up the beach by a steel winch. The first people I've spoken to for hours, they told me of catching fish with giant tumours and of fish that glow slightly in the dark. Here, the blessings of Thatcher's acid reign had fallen not on fishermen but on the kind of vandals who didn't care tuppence, give or take the odd billion, what damage they did.

There was power here to punch a hole clear through to the core, to the very heart of the earth, and to make of it a dead sun to oppose the living one that feeds all natural life. This was the dragon's lair. This black box held all the monsters of wind, rain, famine and plague – its low, throbbing current alternating the benefits of heat and light with danger and a poison more bitter than any rattlesnake's.

Now I recognized the impulse which had brought me to Suffolk looking for an old car. It was only the thin end of a longing for the old days when heroes bubbled up, fountain-wise, into legend. It was a longing for a world where the craftsman, the nomad, the poet, the warrior and the wise man still had a real place. Once there was a wide world, incon-ceivably different from our own – a world of villages and encampments, hermits and brotherhoods – a world where language, music, dancing, ritual, laws and hierarchy both expressed and evoked a living force which I refuse to name.

On that day there was no sunbathed village with wind and clouds moving over it, no meadows and running water, rivers and woods. The trees were chained by their roots to rocks. There was a sorrowful look in the eyes of cows, resignation in the horses. There were luminous fish with tumours and frozen, half-starved birds. I was as lost as them. I looked along the ground or up in the air, dumb and blind as a puppy.

I had spent many days alone because I seemed to get nowhere with people unless I reflected back at them what they already knew – the probable, the common-place, newspapers, TV. Talk of 'searching for the truth' caused the cold shadow of embarrassment and estrangement to pass over even my friends' faces. In the childlike hope of someone to share my unspoken insights I filled up notebooks with hymn-like raptures to the intuitive world. But I didn't dare to expose them or risk the attempt to catch the ear of a world that sells its birthright for a mess of disc-onnected facts and bytes of fast food.

I felt myself moving through ideas and wild imaginings the way that I used to move through places and countries. Inside me there was a spirit or, at least, a spectre, that was struggling to hold its own amid all the chaos and the crap.

I turned slowly as behind me something stirred. Beneath some fishing nets, the black tarpaulin in the back of one of the boats was beginning to move. A figure, deformed and dancing, wavering and trembling stood almost within reach. The tattered form was more like a shadow. It was a ghost, hungry and sick-looking, with eyes, like those of startled rabbits, that were holes in its white-powdered face.

I was terrified. I'd just seen a ghost that looked like me. But the ghost looked far more frightened, because for the first time it had seen someone alive that resembled it and now it realized, for the first time, that it was dead. There was a shock of mutual recognition and the realization that we were both aspects of the same being. The ghost saw the life it was missing and I saw how I lived like a ghost.

I recognized our world of ghosts, where all our gestures have something jerky or inharmonious about them, where the grain of the paper and the coolness on the back of our hands goes unnoticed. I saw how I had been drifting along there with the other ghosts, our anxious faces creased with worry about waistlines and deadlines, hemlines and headlines. I was swayed with the other ghosts by expert opinion or celebrity choice. I was driven by duty or ambition, pulled this way and that. We grinned at each other while we sat together in restaurants and mechanically lifted cooked leaves and roots and slices of animal to our mouths and let them slide into our guts. Stirred, but not shaken enough, we washed down cocktails of amnesia with a glassy cheeriness. We ghosts were as two-dimensional as the magazine world we lived in, where we huddled together in tribes and secretly worried what the others' opinion of us might be.

My ghastly twin had given me time to reflect. But it managed only to draw me deeper into itself. The empty eyes that stared from the shadow were giving out nothing but beginning instead to draw my vital energy from me. At first the voice was only an icy, wheezing rasp. Then he was able to tug out some words. The voice scared me because it sounded so cultured. Awfully, mockingly he began to recite:

> *Things fall apart, the centre cannot hold;*
> *Mere anarchy is loosed upon the world,*
> *The blood-dimmed tide is loosed, and everywhere*
> *The ceremony of innocence is drowned;*
> *The best lack all conviction, while the worst*
> *Are full of passionate intensity.*

'Enough!' I lunged at the phantom, stumbling forward to choke the senselessness out of it. It billowed up over me like a great, black flag, but only for a moment, as it shrank back and shuddered. I caught it in my hands but it slipped through my fingers, turned and fled. It flapped and blew out on to the sea.

I dragged one of the small boats down the shingle and into the sea, then heaved myself in and began rowing towards a patch of water where the waves were being whipped into a cold spray. The silver spray silhouetted a dark shape which could only just be seen. Moving about on the water it made the waves hiss and spit. It was coming at me like some amphetamine-crazed punk. A few feet from the boat it stopped.

'Deep End Club Meeting!' I shouted as I launched myself at him.

As before, the shadow reared up then slithered down and sank, and struck at me from below in a great wave that swelled and swept up and threw the boat clean up out of the water and brought it smashing down hard on top of us. A tumult of water streamed around us, under us and over us, salt-blinding and choking. I gripped him even as he gripped me and we went down together as I dragged him with the weight of my own body and my own death, down with the enormous pull into the deepness of the sea.

The cold currents cracked my limbs. Water surged into my mouth. My head was swelling and my lungs were breaking open. Soon they went light and easy and I no longer needed to breathe. Then the darkness itself cracked with a bursting green light, and the solid, heavy blue gave way to a luminous movement, in which hundreds of fish poised motionless and then swerved away like flakes of silver shooting through the water.

I hung in the old depths, the currents bending and enfolding me. I had fish eyes now. They saw everything. Hundreds of little eyes circled about me. And then hundreds of little i's like children on a carousel, or like a busload of blurred faces peering through a wet window as it passed. But they were all me. Rising, sinking, changing, my whole life began to swim in front of me and flash past: the vision of the drowning man.

There would be no point in justifying all the lifeless, grinning and silly selves. There I was looking ridiculous. There I was angry. And there I was confused. There was a familiar figure being mean and sarcastic. There I was with a face flushed and dulled by drinking. Here was one who wanted money in the bank alongside another who longed to move on a whim and live on his wits. Here was one who felt isolated and alone alongside another who claimed to want nothing to do with people and their stupid ways. Here an immature fear of dying went along with a world-weary readiness to be rid of it all.

But my life had already been lost. It had been stolen by the same trivial forces and common failings which I lost no time in finding in everyone else. All the accusations had become confession.

I went round and round in a circle running after promises, chased by memories and regret. It was a circle in which nothing led anywhere except right back to itself. It churned up a whirlpool of passion and futile argument that threw me first up and then down. Daydreams, ambition, anxieties, self-pity and all the rest of it floated around me like the contents of a thousand ghastly novels. Were these ghosts of the past, or the shadows that future events cast before themselves? It made no difference.

It was terrifying, reassuring and comical: there was nothing apart from a constant shifting undertow of thoughts and moods that brought these characters to life. They used my body and my name coming and going according to circumstance. At this moment alone did something watch over it all

170

and accept the truth. Miraculously in the midst of all this movement something was anchored, indestructible.

All my travels had been only the minutest part of the journey across being. One day I would be returned to my natural condition of ecstasy, back to the centre where everything known and unknown might be found. I would enter the silent, liquid heart where energy had not yet chosen what form it was to take and where what can be sensed and felt had yet to choose whether to be sound or light or thought. Here, before energy was ordered and patterned, and before the simple became complex, I might hear stars, or see the wind. Life would no longer be a complete mystery to me. It would be a mystery complete.

From here I could burst through the well-spring of life, helter-skelter round coils of DNA. I could accelerate towards the distant constellations or sink into the unimaginable vastness and boundless energy of the sea – either way. In either direction I would meet the deep blue mystery.

As the mystery turned itself inside out and burst in an overwhelming and monstrous headlong rush, I flew among a million darting clusters of light where each silver fish flashed like a starry world. The surge took me back up. Over and over it rolled me and flung me like a bit of driftwood on to the rocks.

There I lay, with the unmoving gaze of strange stars on my back, while the waves made a few last efforts to take me back into the sea.

After a long time, I got up slowly on to my hands and knees and crawled away from the water. This brought some warmth back into my body and soon I managed to get to my feet. The darkness was lifting. Then I saw, lined up along the shore in uneven ranks, other boats. It was a strange fleet. The boats appeared to have come from all kinds of places and times. The most ancient of the ships were so encrusted with salt and clinging things that they could hardly be identified. They had fallen to ruin and, like corpses, they calmly endured the slow disintegration that awaits every empty shell.

I walked along the shore. Soon I could see the power station. But there was no black, concrete monolith. It was a pile of old wellington boots built as high as any skyscraper.

Nearer, I could see, set into the black rubber walls at ground level, windows: shop windows. Behind the glass, through the stains and the slime I recognized the names: Nikon, Sony, Rolex. As I approached, one of the cameras clicked into motor drive and fired off a series of shots. I could see that the watches had hands that didn't move. Time stood still. If this was eternity, then you would expect it to.

Inside the shops there were dozens of TVs. But they were all broken in some way. Every one of them had been hurled to its death from the window of a hotel room. Sparks showered from some of them, while others gave a belch of acrid smoke as they flickered back to life. One of the sets showed a picture of clothes churning around inside it, as if it were a washing machine. Other televisions switched back and forth between episodes of 'All My Children' and 'The Love Boat'. The water around them gathered the soap leaking from them. It was churned into a dull, brackish lather by the windmills and waterwheels of the commercial breaks. They continued to show me this make-believe world of good old days, full of images of security, tempting me to hide inside the past again if I was unable or unwilling to find a way forward.

One of the sets clicked into its final rinse and spin. Another repetitively cackled the challenge to save the world, before it clicked like a fruit machine and sent its jackpot spilling on to the sand. There was enough money there to sink a ship.

For a moment I thought I heard music. It stirred a feeling at once carefree and sad. As I neared the place it was coming from I realized that there was someone playing on instruments that I didn't recognize at first, because of the way they blended into something unheard before. This music was so simple it penetrated straight into me.

In an open space there were people, some young and some not so young, tracing the steps of a kind of dance. But the movements were too different to be just a dance. Sometimes they were soft and flowing, at other times precise and complex. At one moment they spun like dervishes, each one turning around the central axis of his own body, orbiting his own spine. Then at the next moment they traced the footwork and the blocks and strikes of some unknown warrior discipline or forgotten martial art.

Although the group moved with an almost miraculous coordination, each dancer appeared to be completely free; provided, so it seemed, that some extraordinary force of attention could be maintained to somehow unify the body, the will and the emotions, and make these movements possible. It was as if each accurate movement of a muscle was almost a sacrament.

Soon I was near enough to the dancers to recognize one of them. I didn't recognize her by her face but by the way she moved – youthful and steady, but full of suppleness. She almost glided, making no effort beyond what was essential. Her movements flowed together in unison with something I could only guess at. Almost instinctively I held out my hand in greeting.

Then I saw the Indian in his feathered head-dress. He rode towards me on his bicycle.

# 11

There was something familiar about the sound of the place, though not quite recognized. No, it was recognized but it couldn't yet be named. Because nothing was identified yet, I was unable to place myself. The scaffolding that normally held up my identity had been demolished.

'Windscreen wiper, speedometer, tired –'

Now, as my eyes opened, some automatic process started silently naming the things that were recognized. For a moment this process was seen as it happened, but then thinking about it made it go somewhere else. I stretched each limb, or rather, as each arm and leg stretched in turn and added itself to my awareness, they literally re-membered me.

This was how I woke up as the bus was pulling into the hotel. We'd arrived in Boulder.

It was early, or late, depending on how you look at it. I wanted some clean sheets and some rest. Without putting down any of my luggage, I banged open the plate glass doors and wedged a foot in the gap and then rolled through in one movement dragging my cases behind me. It was a well-practised move, automatic in places that didn't have automatic doors. This was a posh hotel: the desk clerk's jacket and tie were colour coordinated with the wallpaper and curtains.

There was a discrepancy in our reservation – no record of our booking. People were tired. Tempers frayed. The night clerk was insulted more and more. A security man arrived and we very nearly didn't get in at all.

At last I got to my room. The very moment that I put my bag down, music started up in the room next door. What was the matter with these people! I banged on the wall and shouted threats but to no avail. Downstairs at the front desk I had to use every ounce of sympathy, persuasion, explanation, cajoling and coaxing to try and get the desk clerk to change my room for another. I gave him twenty bucks. He gave me the new key.

'Ya see,' he said, still smouldering with indignation, 'I don't have to take that kinda shit from you people.'

'You just did, pal,' I replied. Now that was worth twenty dollars. But in the same instant I regretted saying it.

All the time there was this contradiction in me, this separation: one 'I' said something, another regretted it. It was as if everything I did belonged to other people; yet being aware of this separation had something about it that felt much closer to reality, not further away.

I went back upstairs and collected my luggage. It was positively uncanny: the very moment I picked up my bag the music stopped. I struggled down two floors carrying all my stuff in one go, opened the door of my new room and set down my luggage. Music started. Then it began to dawn. I picked the bag up; the music stopped. I put the bag down; the music started again. Carefully unzipping the bag I looked inside and, repeating the experiment, saw how the wine bottle was resting on the switch that turned the radio of my cassette player on and off as I picked up the bag and put it down. I switched it off and went to the bathroom.

Someone began revving up a Harley Davidson. No, it was only the air conditioner that had come on with the bathroom light. I tore away the strip of paper from the toilet seat –

'sanified for your comfort and protection'. Then I knocked over the plastic tumbler into which I'd just put my toothbrush and razor and sent them clattering and scattering into the bath. With more than a shade of impatience, I picked everything up and replaced it in the tumbler. Five seconds later I knocked the whole lot flying again, this time managing to take a star-shaped chip out of the enamel of the bath.

That record labelled irritation was on the turntable again, just as it had been earlier in the morning, I mean yesterday morning, I mean ... 'comfort and protection' from what, anyway? Was there some madman or some phantom, lurking in the bowl, held back only by this paper talisman and ready to burst forth in a fountain of toilet water with a peculiar and poisonous outlook that would flood the place? There was an awful shock of recognition.

I lay down on the bed for a while without getting undressed. I felt all scaly and twitchy from having had to sit for too long, and when I closed my eyes I saw headlights: round, luminous blobs that became fishes' eyes. I walked over to the window and out on to a small balcony. The sun would soon be up. I'd go out and watch it, walk around for a while, then sleep through the morning. Maybe I'd see if I could hire a bike for a couple of hours before it was time to do the soundcheck. The early morning is the best time of the day; I saw it barely once or twice a month.

Outside, I walked away and away from the hotel, along the edge of the freeway, towards the higher ground. The light spread slowly, as if coming on foot, gradually flushing out a shadow here, filling in a colour there. Frost still lay in little patches at the edge of the road; it sparkled on the bodies of the parked cars and I saw the vapour from my breath rise in front of me. An eighteen-wheeler blundered along, belching black diesel fumes. It was closely followed by an old convertible, which swung boldly past and sped away to where the highway narrowed into a thread and the hills made some beauty out of the distance. It was one of those times, and places, where light and air begin to wake up the senses so that the mind, tired from too much of itself, slows down: when there is almost no end to how far you can see.

As I walked away from the road the sun broke through, making a patch of light dance over the contours of the land. As my gaze followed it, it looked as if small, green fires were bursting out from between the iron rock. I turned and saw the sun sparkling, not silver, but white gold, on the bright metal panels of our bus, over a mile away now. A bird wheeled and turned like a flake fallen from one of the clouds. A beautiful grey snake lay killed in the sand.

Though I was now carrying some new questions, in a way these questions themselves were half-way to being answers. The spirit that moves us to look for the truth, is the very truth we are looking for.

I took advantage of a spur of rising ground, where sun-parched grass hung in pale strands, and began to climb. Soon the slope steepened and I half-scrambled over the loose stones and scrub until, like the wild oaks, I was having to struggle to get a foothold on the side of the hill. Once I was out of sight of the highway I was back where the Indians walked.

I stopped to sit for a minute or two.

After a while there was a subtle change in the atmosphere that brought me the most vivid impression of myself simply sitting there. It caught me by surprise, because no matter where I looked I found the sensations becoming richer and richer, pulse by pulse and wave by wave. It was happening so swiftly that I had no power of attention which could keep up with it. It was a silence that was charged and alive and aware of itself that rang all around me now, while every little sound and detail struck me immediately, light and direct. I was filled with thanks for the present. I accepted the gift of a rare and precious awareness that all life is new: a moment of simple witnessing of myself in life and life in myself, together.

A healing stillness had filled me and spread to the seething and radiant elements around me like rings from a stone dropped in water. And while I was at the centre, the centre was everywhere. Everything was shot through with this peculiar new energy. It spread over the surfaces. It slid over the rocks and flowed through gullies. It piled up beneath the sky and snapped over ridges. It fell like rain on the back of my neck. It swarmed through my plexus and pricked the hairs as it fluttered over my skin like warm air over a summer field.

An insect, almost transparent, set down on a stalk of grass by my foot. I watched it flex its wings. From above I must have looked much the same.

# Backword

I am back home in London. It is getting on for three years since the group split up.

I am just about to go downstairs to take Angus for his late afternoon walk when the phone rings. It is an American friend of mine who plays with B B King's band. They are here for a short British tour.

(Last night I had been with some friends to see him play at Hammersmith Odeon. Afterwards we were all going to an Indian restaurant. The others went on ahead while I went backstage to collect my buddy and bring him along when he'd changed out of his shiny, mohair suit and the shirt with the big collar.

'Oh man, I was really out of it up there tonight,' he said, looking round to make sure nobody would overhear him. 'I mean, I was really flaking. This is one tired guy.'

'It sounded great to me,' I said, making no secret of the fact that I was a fan of his boss. 'I got the tingles up the back again. He can still do it. Thirty, forty years on the road and he still keeps coming up with something. How does he do it?'

'You know, I think it's starting to catch up with him.'

'What about you?' I asked my buddy.

'I'm just tryin' to get some money in the bank, save as much as I can. Trouble is –'

'Yeah, I know. Anyway are you ready? The car's parked a

few streets away. Do you mind a walk, or shall I drive it round and give you a blast on the horn?'

For a few seconds it looked as if he was considering the option. 'Listen man, I think I need to get to the hotel and just rest up a bit, shake off this lag. I'll call you tomorrow.')

'Heeeyyyyeah.' His Tennessee drawl has a way of making one word sound like a sentence.

'How y'doin'?' I say. 'Did you get a good rest? Sorry you didn't make it out with us last night.'

'Well, you know man,' he says, as if it needs no explaining. And really, it doesn't.

'Did you get up early and go out, like you said?' I laugh.

'No man. But I've had a great day.'

'How's that?'

'I found me a laundromat near the hotel. I had four of them machines all goin' at once. I got all my laundry done,' he says with plain satisfaction.

'You could have come over and put it all in our machine,' I say.

'Hey, maybe I'll take you up on that sometime.'

His band have already been out on this latest tour for two months. A few days ago they completed the Australian leg of the tour, took a 27-hour flight straight to London and then went directly from Heathrow to the BBC to record a TV show. They have fourteen gigs in the UK in as many days and then fly straight to another in Grand Rapids, Michigan; then Detroit, then –

'New Orleans, Japan, Europe –'

My buddy is reading through the itinerary, turning over a handful of pages at a time.

'Do you wanna go some place tonight to eat, or come over

for a drink or something?' I suggest. 'We'll make sure you get back to the hotel.'

There is a long pause. 'Y'know man, we've got to be up real early to go to Dublin –'

'You know what,' I interrupt.

'What?'

'You're getting roadbound,' I laugh.

'Yeah. You're startin' to miss it, eh?'

He takes me completely by surprise because I realize that I've actually forgotten what it feels like, to feel like he does right now. There's only a memory.

'OK then,' I recover. 'After Dublin what is it – Liverpool, Manchester?'

'Yeah, then Edinburgh, Leeds, Croydon, Port's Mouth –'

'Can you get me a couple of tickets and passes an' I'll come down to Croydon.'

'Yeah, great. Then maybe we can have a drink and a yarn back at the hotel, or somethin'.'

'Sure.'

'Anyway, how's your day bin?' says my buddy.

'I've been writing,' I reply.

'What you writing, songs an' shit?'

'I'm writing, well, I guess it's a bit like what we're talking about,' I say.

'Well, I won't keep you from it any longer.' He sounds both puzzled and, for some reason, polite.

'OK. Have a good one tonight and I'll give you a call in Croydon. See ya next week.'

I turn to go downstairs when the phone rings again. It's the Drummer. He's calling with details of some session work we may be doing later in the month.

'Got anything on at the moment?' I ask.

'I'm doing something with Big George. He's getting a band together for a show on Sky channel, but it's all a bit up in the air –'

'Well it would be.'

'What d'you mean?' says the Drummer and then he laughs quite openly at the awful pun as it reveals itself to him. I'm glad to see that two years of not drinking is not diminishing his sense of humour.

'What's Norman up to at the moment?' I ask. (The Keyboard Player has gained yet another alias.)

'A yoghurt ad. And he's doing the soundtrack for some documentary about the ozone layer or the rain forests, or something. That should score him a few grave points. And his chocolate jingle's out.'

'What's that?'

'Haven't you heard it!' says the Drummer. 'It's on nearly every night. And that's him at the end shouting, "I want more milk chocolate Skittles!"'

We finish speaking.

Although I have no reason to speak to the Singer right now, just to round things off and to see if he's having any luck with his new career as a folk singer, I dial his number.

An answering machine clicks on. In a hammy, East European accent his voice announces, 'You have just reached the Bulgarian Embassy. If you would like to leave your name and number we will arrange for one of our staff to come round and visit you with one of our special umbrellas.'

For a minute, I just sit; trying to sit still, relaxed and upright – as empty and impressionable as a fresh sheet of paper. The window is open and though my eyes are closed I am awake.

The serious business of having nothing in mind is not a passive state.

In the near distance a train rolls along clacking rails. In a room next door a decorator sands down some paintwork in a regular rhythm. The two sounds combine to evoke a memory of the steam trains that used to pass the house I lived in as a boy. Watching actively, listening with attention, I don't get coupled to that train of thought. Committed to staying awake, I let thoughts, opinions, memories, stories, enter into my vision and then float past, like clouds, simply observed. Neither do the sounds of jets approaching the airport send me on any more flights of fancy. In a way their sound, settling in the sky, serves only to confirm the peace – charged and alive, continual and unbroken – that lies behind everything, everywhere.

Now, from downstairs, crockery and cutlery are heard rattling against each other, like all the other things that come and go in the face of what is. Any moment this naked does not feel secure or predictable. But it might be the perfect place to –

'Angus? Walkies!'